A SPECIAL NOTE

Designed with the do-it-yourself enthusiast in
mind, this book's special wire binding enables
you to use it where you need it most—right at
your workbench. Pages lie perfectly flat; there's
never a problem with irritating flip-overs.

REVISED
and
EXPANDED

Newest Ways
TO EXPERT WOODWORKING

**EASY Power Tool Techniques for All Do-It-Yourself Materials
Including Wood, Aluminum, Composition Materials, Tile and Plastics.
Plus portable power tool uses and new home shop ideas.**

by the EDITORIAL BOARD of

B&D DeWALT

The Black & Decker Manufacturing Company

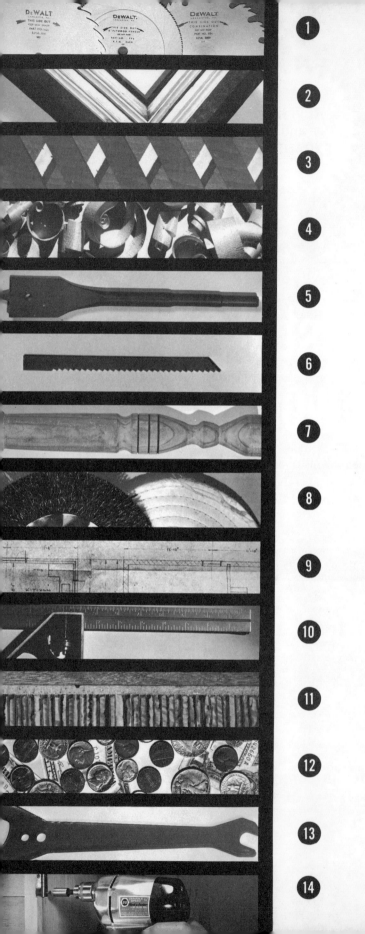

CONTENTS

CREDITS

The Editorial Board wishes to extend thanks to the following organizations for their co-operative attitude in preparing this revised edition.

AMERICAN HOME MAGAZINE—*New York, New York*
AMERICAN BUILDER MAGAZINE—*New York, New York*
ARMSTRONG CORK COMPANY—*Lancaster, Pennsylvania*
AMERICAN PLYWOOD ASSOCIATION—*Tacoma, Washington*
E. I. DUPONT DE NEMOURS & CO.—*Wilmington, Delaware*
MASONITE CORPORATION—*Chicago, Illinois*
POPULAR SCIENCE MONTHLY MAGAZINE—*New York, New York*
UNITED STATES PLYWOOD ASSOCIATION—*New York, New York*

Also, we wish to express our appreciation to the following specialists and company associates for their knowledge and personal guidance that make this revision authorative and up-to-date.

Eugene V. Allen	A. Allan Noe
Marlin R. Boyer	Herbert R. Pfister
L. E. Brizzolara, Jr.	Robert Scharff
Kenneth K. Kittinger	H. (Pete) Smith
Jack Long	J. H. Yoakum

Also, our sincere thanks for the numerous requests from our dealer organizations and customers, that prompted the original edition of *Newest Ways to Expert Woodworking*, as well as this second major revision.

Happy Woodworking!

Wm. F. Kinderwater
Co-ordinator, Editorial Board
THE BLACK & DECKER MANUFACTURING COMPANY

CHAPTER 1

INTRODUCTION TO THE RADIAL-ARM MACHINE

The ever-increasing popularity of woodworking as a relaxing and rewarding pastime bears witness to the fact that it is one of the most lasting and satisfying endeavors a person can undertake. Wood appeals to the craftsman because of the ease with which it can be fashioned into thousands of useful products. It can be cut into any desired shape, drilled, sanded, and finished with a variety of woodworking tools.

There are over 6,000 known uses for wood, ranging from toothpicks to structural members in industrial building. This flexibility has led to the development of versatile tools of many different designs and types, each of which offers one or more features to satisfy a specific need.

Thousands of homecraftsmen and hobbyists have discovered that a radial-arm machine adds professional scope and skill to their work. They learned what builders and manufacturers have known for many years: for utility, versatility, and safety you can't beat a radial-arm machine. This amazing multi-purpose machine, when equipped with the proper attachments, is really 15 tools in one—capable of performing literally hundreds of operations.

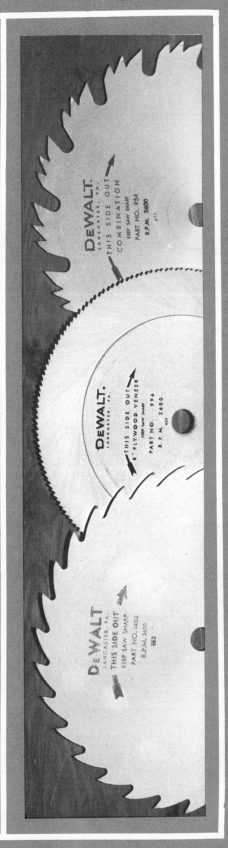

The first radial-arm machine was originated and perfected by Raymond E. DeWalt in 1922 for the purpose of providing more versatility and safety in woodworking. The following year, he and a few associates began production of the machine shown at the left. The modern radial-arm machine, manufactured by the company still bearing Mr. DeWalt's name, is shown at the bottom. While the machine has changed greatly in appearance, it still offers the amazing versatility and safety of the original model, plus a great deal more.

As you can see by the table of contents, it is a complete workshop. It will saw, dado, and shape with complete accuracy. (These operations comprise 85 per cent of all homeshop work.) With the proper attachments added, it will function as a jointer, drill, router, saber saw, lathe, sander (disc and drum), grinder, buffer, and polisher. The radial-arm machine's versatility also extends into

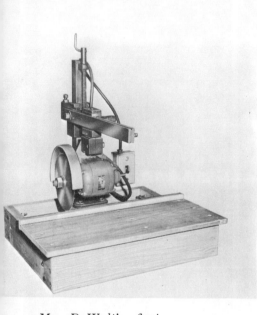

Mr. DeWalt's first radial-arm machine.

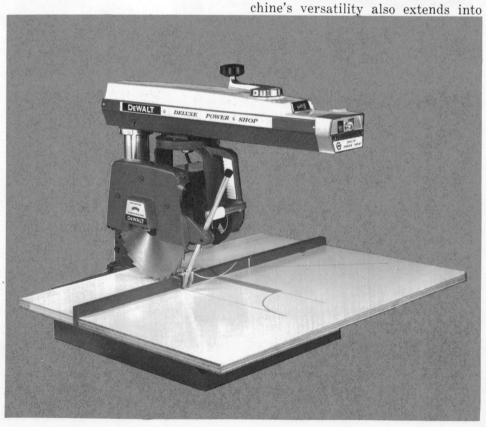

the working of new building materials (see Chapter 11) such as hardboard, plywood, fiberboard, floor covering, acoustical tile, do-it-yourself aluminum, etc.

Such built-in features as the removable key-lock switch and push-button starting arrangement, the large work table, which eliminates saw overhang, totally enclosed fan cooled direct drive motor, the rubber dust spout which directs chips away from the operator, the saw blade guard with the anti-kickback device attached, king size control knobs, an automatic brake which stops the rotation of the cutting tool seconds after shut-off, and the basic machine design which places all moving parts above the work surface in easy view of the operator—all combine to make the radial-arm machine illustrated throughout this book the standard of safety by which other power tools are evaluated.

Flexibility with this tool means that the cutting member can be placed in any position throughout all three dimensions — length, width, and depth. This is possible because its unique design allows full maneuverability through a complete circle in any of three directions. With so flexible a machine, you'll be performing operations you never thought possible. On the other hand, if you have just one operation to perform, the radial-arm machine will do it as efficiently as any single-purpose tool. And if a change in your design or a change in your method takes place, the radial-arm machine can be changed quickly to perform the new job with equal efficiency. In the following chapters, you'll see how easily this modern machine can be operated and what savings can be effected in your working time.

SHOULDER ACTION. The radial arm (A)—from which this type of machine derives its name—rotates 180° or 360° depending on the model, for right- or left-miter cuts. Merely release clamp (B), then swing arm to desired angle. The eye-level calibrated miter scale (D) shows you the miter angle you want. The "built-in" stops at 0° and 45° will help you locate these common angles. You never shift the lumber for miters—just put the saw at the required angle and pull across for perfect cuts every time. An accurate measuring scale, on the right side of the arm, gives you measurements for ripping. Another part of the shoulder action is the fact that the mechanical arm can be raised or lowered. Each full turn of the elevating handle (C) raises or lowers the arm (A) exactly 1/8-inch. One-half turn gives you 1/16 inch. One-eighth of a turn (marked on the arm) gives you 1/64 inch. This is a precision depth control.

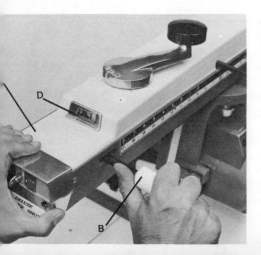

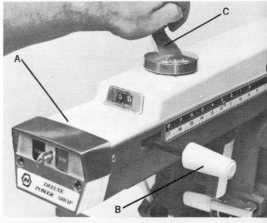

ELBOW ACTION. In the elbow action of the mechanical arm, the yoke, which holds the motor, is beneath the arm and rides freely on it. Pull the yoke clamp (E) forward, unlocking the yoke. Pull the handle farther forward, striking the cam cup (F), which releases the locating pin. Then swing the yoke right or left. It automatically stops at all four 90° positions, giving you quick, positive adjustment for ripping and cross-cutting.

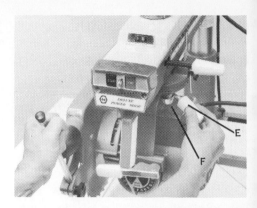

WRIST ACTION. To see the wrist movement of the mechanical arm, pull out the clamp (G) which unlocks the bevel lock and automatically releases the locating pin (H). Tilt the motor (I) for the angle desired on the bevel scale (J). Relock G. The locating pin automatically locates the 0°, 45°, and 90° bevel positions. Your compound angles and bevel cuts are measured for you with unequaled accuracy, and there is no limit to the bevel cut angle. To work with this machine, all you have to remember is that its flexible operation is based on three simple radial adjustments. The *arm* can be swung horizontally through 180° or 360°, depending on the model, around its column; the *yoke* can be revolved horizontally through 360° under its roller carriage; and the motor can be tilted within the yoke to any angle desired. These three adjustments enable you to place the cutting tool easily in any position.

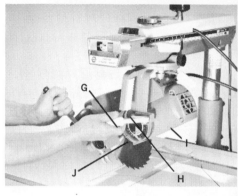

RADIAL-ARM MACHINE SIZES. Before being designed for homeshop use, the radial-arm machine had a remarkable industrial safety record, and this is one of the many reasons why it is replacing, more and more, the so-called table saw, which was for many years a standard item of equipment in most home, school, and industrial shops. Radial-arm machines are available in sizes ranging from $1\frac{1}{4}$ to 10 horsepower. The most popular builder model is shown here, while the home workshop model is illustrated throughout this book. This machine which delivers over $2\frac{1}{4}$ horsepower, cuts 3 inches deep with a 10-inch blade, crosscuts pieces up to $14\frac{1}{2}$ inches wide on 1-inch stock, and rips to a maximum width of $24\frac{7}{8}$ inches.

CONNECTING THE MACHINE TO THE POWER SUPPLY. The radial-arm machine may be mounted on saw horses (temporary installation), on a steel cabinet or legs, or built into a workbench (see Chapter 9). The machine is uncrated and assembled according to the manufacturer's instructions furnished with it. To obtain the maximum efficiency from your machine's motor, the wire from the source of power to the machine should not be less than size 14 (B and S gauge). Be sure the electric line is fused with a 15-ampere fuse. If an ordinary fuse blows during the initial fraction of a second after the machine is turned on, don't put in a new one of higher rating. Instead, replace it with a fuse of the same rating, but of the "slow-blow" or delay type. It contains a special fusible link that withstands a momentary overload without giving way. The radial-arm machine, as any other power tool, should always be grounded while in use. This precaution will protect the operator against possible electric shock should a short circuit or ground develop while the machine is being connected to the power outlet, or during operation. The radial-arm machine offers new and assured grounding protection for your safety. In accordance with a ruling of the National Electric Code, it is equipped with a three-wire cord, one wire being a ground wire. If your power outlet isn't 3-prong grounded type, use a standard adaptor. To start the machine, insert key, unlock the push button switch (above left) and you're ready for a lifetime of woodworking pleasure. The machine's motor is protected against overloading by a manual-reset Klixon thermostat which kicks out when the motor is overheated. To reset the motor, turn off the switch, wait 10 minutes, then "push in" the red button on the motor (above).

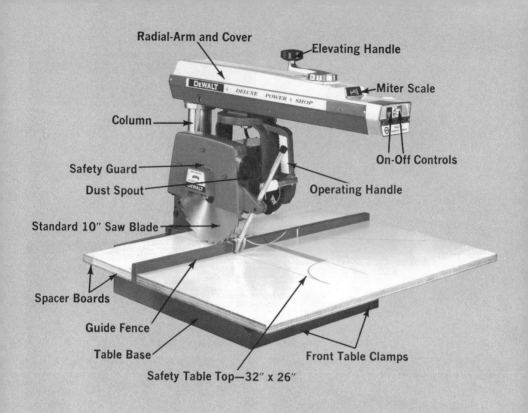

Radial-Arm and Cover
Elevating Handle
Miter Scale
Column
On-Off Controls
Safety Guard
Dust Spout
Operating Handle
Standard 10" Saw Blade
Spacer Boards
Guide Fence
Table Base
Front Table Clamps
Safety Table Top—32" x 26"

RADIAL-ARM MACHINE CONTROLS. The versatility of the radial-arm machine is due, in part, to its controls, and these are the keys to its successful operation. Learn to use them by adjusting the machine for all operations before actually starting to operate it. All controls, as well as the major parts of the radial-arm machine, are shown and identified here.

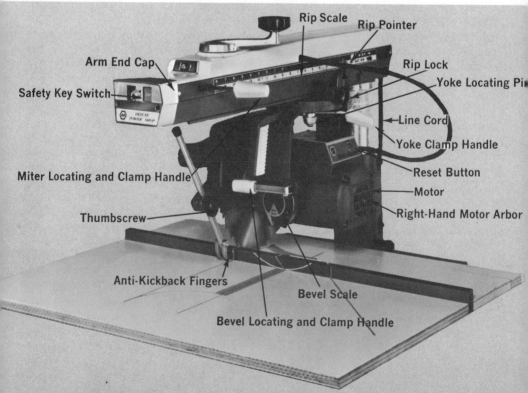

Rip Scale
Rip Pointer
Arm End Cap
Rip Lock
Yoke Locating Pin
Safety Key Switch
Line Cord
Yoke Clamp Handle
Miter Locating and Clamp Handle
Reset Button
Motor
Thumbscrew
Right-Hand Motor Arbor
Anti-Kickback Fingers
Bevel Scale
Bevel Locating and Clamp Handle

CHAPTER 2

SAWING

Have you ever stopped to think how many different kinds of saw cuts there are? Actually there are only six basic saw cuts in woodworking—crosscut, bevel crosscut, miter, bevel miter, rip, and, bevel rip. All other saw cuts, no matter how intricate, are combinations of these basic cuts.

With a radial-arm saw, the basic cuts are safe and easy. Because the blade is above the table top, you are always working on top of the material, with layout marks in clear view. The saw is never hidden beneath the material—you always know where it is. The saw also adjusts to the lumber for all cuts—no need to shift the wood when changing operations from cross to miter to rip, etc. With the material in a stationary position, your hands are safely away from the blade.

The radial-arm machine is a pull-through saw and uses climb feed for cutting. In this action, the saw blade is moved in the same direction as its rotation. This means the saw's thrust against the work is down and to the rear. Material placed against the guide fence is held there by the blade's action. Although it is possible to crosscut material as small as ¾ by 1 inch without holding, the recommended procedure is to steady the material with your hand or support it by pressing another piece of wood against it while the cut is being made.

When ripping, or cutting with the

grain, on the radial-arm machine you must *never* feed the work into the saw blade in the same direction as it is rotating. Remember, the radial-arm saw operates on a climb-feed principle. When ripping you must feed into the rotation of the blade (see pages 24, 25 and 26).

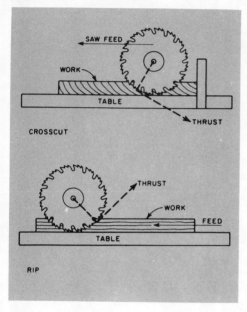

The radial-arm saw is one of the safest power tools ever made. However, with any tool, certain precautions must be taken. Before operating the saw, read the following rules carefully—for your safety—and remember them always.

■ Be sure the blade is mounted properly and is held securely in place by the arbor nut.

■ Always use the safety guard with the proper adjustment when operating the machine.

■ Be sure all clamp and locking handles are tight.

■ The saw should always be returned to the rear of the table after completing a cross or miter cut.

■ The equipment should be shut off when making any adjustment.

■ The saw blade or tools should be completely stopped before you leave the machine.

■ When cutting material, the stock should always lie flat on the table and be held firmly against the guide fence. Don't force material into the saw or stall the motor.

■ Stock should not be removed from the table until the saw has been returned to the rear of the table.

■ Always use a stick to remove small pieces of scrap from the worktable. Never get your hands in the path of the saw's travel.

■ The worktable should always be kept clean—no loose material should be left on it.

■ When ripping, the direction of rotation of the saw blade will be toward the operator. Always feed the material past the safety guard from the side opposite the anti-kickback fingers. (Observe the caution tag on the safety guard.) Never stand in back of, or in direct line with, the saw when ripping.

■ When making any cut, keep in a well-balanced position. If crosscutting material from the left, put the left foot forward and place the left hand approximately 12 inches to the left of the saw-blade travel. Pull the yoke handle with the right hand. If cutting from the right side, put the right foot forward and hold the material with the right hand. Pull the yoke handle with the left hand. Never cross your arms when cutting—change hands when changing operations.

■ Always use the anti-kickback assembly when ripping or ploughing.

■ Keep the saw blade sharp. Never use cracked or improper saw blades.

■ Like any power tool, the radial arm will function efficiently and accurately only if you ensure that all components are in the correct relationship to each other. Check the machine, following the manufacturer's instructions, the first time you set it up; check it periodically thereafter (see Chapter 13).

COMMON TYPES OF SAW BLADES.
There are four basic types of saw
blades you should have in your shop.
They are (left to right) combination,
hollow ground, rip and plywood. *Combination Blade:* Your radial-arm saw
usually comes equipped with a combination blade which will make all the
cuts equally well. This blade is adaptable to most home-workshop needs for
general-purpose work. The combination blade is divided into segments
and provides crosscut teeth and one
raker tooth in each segment, with a
deep gullet between. This arrangement permits the blade to cut freely
and smoothly both with and across
the grain. *Hollow-ground Blade:* This
blade generally has four cutting
teeth and one raker, and the teeth
have no set. The blade is beveled, or
hollow-ground, so that it is several
gauges thinner near the hub than at
the rim. Sometimes called a planer
or miter blade, it is generally used by
cabinetmakers when cutting stock to
finished dimensions because it cuts
very smoothly both with and across
the grain and reduces the amount of
sanding required. *Ripping Blade:* The
ripping blade is designed to do just
one job—cutting with the grain of the
wood. The blade tends to tear wood
on crosscuts but cuts fast and clean
when ripping. Since ripping usually
puts a heavy load on the motor, this
blade is recommended for general ripping jobs. *Plywood Blade:* This fine-tooth cutting blade with its thin-rim
taper does an excellent job on plywood and gummy, resinous woods. It
makes cuts with smooth finishes, ideal
for glue joints. Plywood blades are
also available in the thin kerf line
type, for use on both plywoods and
veneers.

**OTHER TYPES OF COMBINATION
BLADES.** In addition to the standard
or novelty tooth flat-ground combination blade described, there are several
other combination blades which may
be used in woodworking. The most
important of these are discussed
here. *Chisel Tooth Flat-ground
Combination Blade:* The teeth are set
for clearance and fast cutting. The
cut, however, isn't as smooth as the
novelty type. *Hard Tip Combination
Blade:* The teeth are set for clearance
and are heat treated for longer life.
They stay sharp longer, but are
harder to resharpen and don't cut as
smoothly as the other combination
blades. *Carbide Tipped Combination
Blade:* The eight-tooth carbide tipped
saw blade rips and crosscuts like any
other combination blade. It remains
sharp for long periods of continuous
operation and outlasts ordinary blades
many times over. It is ideal for cutting hardboard, plywood, asbestos
board, and similar materials. Carbide
blades are more expensive and don't
produce as smooth a cut in the softer
woods as the standard combination
type. *Cabinet Combination Blade:*
This fine tooth type blade is for cutting thin stock up to 1¼ inches and
results in a very smooth cut. There
are two styles of this blade. One is the
thin kerf line type with its 52 teeth
set for clearance, while the other—the
thin-rim taper—has its 52 teeth taper
ground for clearance with raker teeth
to clean out the sawdust. As with all
saw blades, keep them clean and
sharp. To prevent rusting keep them
oiled when not in use.

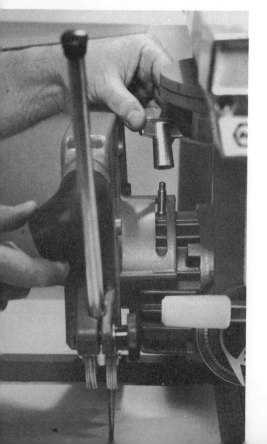

MOUNTING THE SAW BLADE. Remove the arbor nut and arbor collars. Elevate the radial arm until the blade will slide on the shaft and clear the table top. Place one collar on the arbor so the recessed side of the collar will be against the saw blade (top left). Then place the saw blade on the arbor. The teeth of the saw blade must point in the direction of rotation when in the proper operating position. Put on the other arbor collar, recessed side against the blade. Now hold the arbor with the hex wrench and tighten the arbor nut with the arbor-nut wrench (top right). The arbor nut has a left-hand thread, which means the nut must be tightened counter-clockwise. Mount and adjust the safety guard on the motor stud to the desired position for the cuts you are going to make; tighten the wing nut (left).

CROSSCUTTING. For straight crosscutting, the radial arm must be at right angles with the guide fence—indicated as 0° on the miter scale. Locate the miter latch in the column slot at the 0° position, and securely lock the arm with the arm clamp handle. The saw blade should follow the saw kerf in the table top. Use the elevating handle to lower the saw blade until the teeth are approximately $^1/_{16}$ inch below the surface of the table. This clearance is needed to cut through the board. Return the saw all the way back to the column. Place the material against the guide fence. Adjust the guard parallel to the bottom of the motor; adjust the kickback fingers to $^1/_8$ inch above the material to be cut. Turn the power on and give the motor sufficient time to attain top speed. Then pull the saw completely through the cut in one steady motion. Never allow the blade to "walk" too rapidly through the work. Return the saw behind the guide fence before removing the material from the table. To have the saw blade automatically return to the rear of the guide fence, you can install a device such as the "Saf-T-Bak" (bottom) to the rear of the machine arm. This attachment is a must for most school shops and industrial plants.

RIGHT- OR LEFT-HAND FEED. Your first cut will pose the question of whether to use right-hand (below) or left-hand feed (right). You may have a tendency to use left-hand feed because the right hand holds the material on the side away from the saw. However, right-hand feed generally is more practical and more comfortable, and you will quickly adopt this system. The long part of the work should always be on the side of the holding hand. When using right-hand feed, for example, the long part of the material would be on the left since you would be holding it down with the left hand. Be sure to keep the table clean in order to insure even contact between the board and guide fence. The illustration at the right also shows the automatic safety guard in use. This unique guard with "free-floating" action is a practical and absolutely safe solution to enclosing the lower half of the saw blade on a radial-arm machine. The two circular safety rings, which are free to adjust automatically for depth and angle of cut, protect the operator at all times from the cutting member and moving parts of the machine. The guard in no way detracts from the versatility of the machine nor from the maneuverability of the cutting member through all normal woodworking operations. Although designed primarily for use with a wood-cutting saw blade, the new "free-floating" guard can also be used for dado work, accommodating a full-width head.

CROSSCUTTING SIMILAR LENGTHS. When crosscutting more than one piece to the same length, a stop block arrangement, such as shown here, should be employed. Note that a notch is cut on the underside of the block to gather the sawdust so it doesn't impede the accuracy of your cuts (left). You can also cut similar lengths by using the "gang cutting" technique shown below.

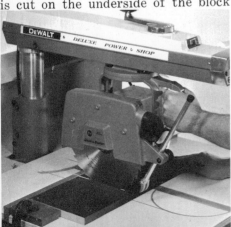

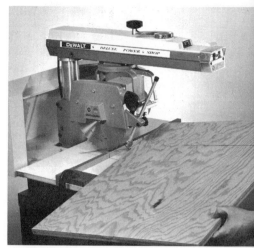

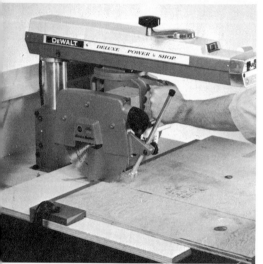

CROSSCUTTING WIDE BOARDS. To cut a board wider than the capacity of the machine, set up a stop block arrangement to be sure two cuts of the same length will be obtained. Then cut as far on one side of the board as you can (top left). Turn the board over and align the kerf using the stop block as a guide (above). To complete the cut, pull the saw through the remainder of material (left).

CROSSCUTTING THICK TIMBERS. To cut a board thicker than the capacity of the machine, set the blade a little over half the thickness of the material. Pull the blade through in the same manner as for straight crosscutting, turn it over and complete the cut on the other side. When turning the material over, line its kerf with the one on the table top to assure a square cut. Unless you are certain that both edges are parallel, turn the piece so the same edge is against the guide fence.

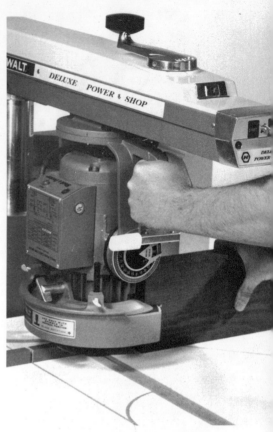

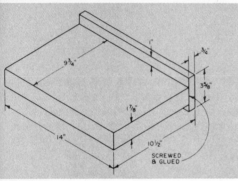

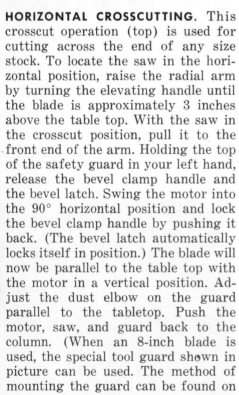

HORIZONTAL CROSSCUTTING. This crosscut operation (top) is used for cutting across the end of any size stock. To locate the saw in the horizontal position, raise the radial arm by turning the elevating handle until the blade is approximately 3 inches above the table top. With the saw in the crosscut position, pull it to the front end of the arm. Holding the top of the safety guard in your left hand, release the bevel clamp handle and the bevel latch. Swing the motor into the 90° horizontal position and lock the bevel clamp handle by pushing it back. (The bevel latch automatically locks itself in position.) The blade will now be parallel to the table top with the motor in a vertical position. Adjust the dust elbow on the guard parallel to the tabletop. Push the motor, saw, and guard back to the column. (When an 8-inch blade is used, the special tool guard shown in picture can be used. The method of mounting the guard can be found on page 46.) Place the material to be cut against the guide fence and lower the saw blade to the point where the cut is to be made. The depth of the cut will be determined by the location of the material in respect to the saw blade. Turn on the motor and pull the saw through the material in the same manner as when crosscutting. When horizontal crosscutting thin stock, it will be necessary to build an auxiliary table and guide fence (shown bottom left) since the width of the safety guard will not allow the blade to be lowered to more than $1\frac{1}{4}$ inches above the stationary table top. The auxiliary table is installed in place of the standard guide fence. To do this, release the two clamp screws, lift out the guide fence, slide in the auxiliary table, and retighten the clamp screws. The material is placed against the auxiliary guide fence and cut as previously described (above).

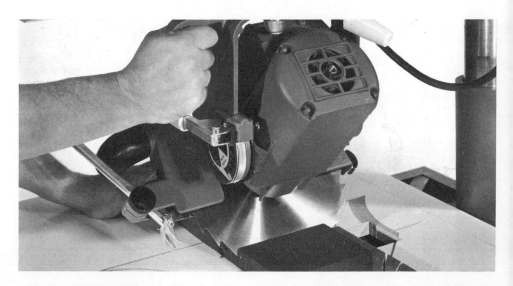

BEVEL CROSSCUTTING. This operation is similar to straight crosscutting, but the saw is tilted to the desired angle. Elevate the machine so the blade will clear the table top when swiveling the motor in the yoke. Pull the motor and saw to the front end of the arm. To bevel the saw, place your left hand on top of the safety guard to keep the motor from dropping and release the bevel clamp lock and locating pin by pulling the handle forward. Move the motor to the degree desired by following the bevel scale and pointer. Lock the bevel clamp by pushing it back. Lower the saw as in regular crosscutting, so the blade is $^1/_{16}$ inch below table surface. Push the motor and saw back to the column. If a 45° bevel is desired, the locating pin will automatically stop at this setting. Then lock the bevel clamp. Place the material on the table top against the guide fence. Adjust the guard as you would in crosscutting.

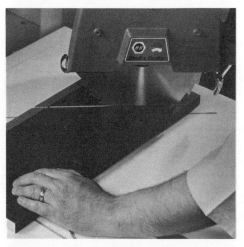

RIGHT-HAND MITERING. Mitering is the same as crosscutting except that the radial arm is revolved on a horizontal plane to the angle of the miter. Be sure the motor and saw blade are in back of the guide fence. With your right hand, pull the arm clamp all the way forward, releasing the arm lock and miter latch. With your left hand on the radial arm, swing it to the right to the angle desired by following the miter scale. Lock the arm clamp handle. The popular 45° miter cut is set quickly with the miter latch seated in the 45° slot in the column. Now place the material flat on the table top and tight against the guide fence. Adjust the guard parallel to the bottom of the motor; adjust the kickback fingers to $\frac{1}{8}$ inch above the material you will be cutting. Hold the material with your left hand, and pull the saw with your right. Return the saw to its original position before removing the material from the table top.

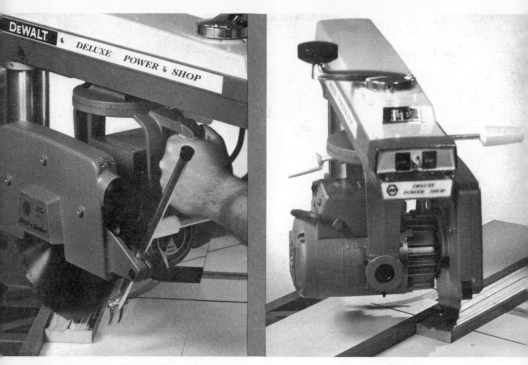

LEFT-HAND MITERING. Move the radial arm to the left to the desired angle in the manner described for a right-hand miter. To get the full capacity for a left-hand miter, move the guide fence to the rear of the table-top spacer boards. To make this adjustment, release the two clamp handles holding the boards, move the guide fence back, and tighten the clamp handles. Place the material to be cut flat on the table top and tight against the guide fence. Adjust the guard and kickback fingers, in the same way as for a right-hand miter cut. With the right hand holding the material, pull the saw and motor through the material with your left hand (above). Then return the motor to its original position. Left-hand miters can also be made by swiveling the motor, yoke, and saw 180° from the standard crosscutting position. With the saw in this position, it is not necessary to reposition the guide fence. This setup is very important when making both left- and right-hand cuts on a molding where it is impossible to reverse the material. To swivel the motor, yoke, and saw blade 180°, raise the column by turning the elevating handle several times; then pull the yoke clamp

forward, unlocking the yoke. Pull the handle farther forward, striking the cam cup, releasing the locating pin. Swivel the yoke clockwise 180°, then lock the clamp handle. With your right hand, release the arm clamp handle by pulling it forward all the way to release the miter latch. Swing the radial arm to the desired left-hand miter position. Tighten the arm clamp handle by pushing it back. With the motor at the front end of the arm, turn the machine on and, with the saw running, lower the blade until it cuts a kerf $1/16$-inch deep in the table top. Then push the saw back through the guide fence to cut a kerf through it. Turn the current off. Since the blade is turning toward you, tilt the safety guard forward so it clears the material you are cutting by approximately $1/16$ inch. With your right hand, hold down the material *tightly* against the guide fence. Since the yoke hand grip is at the rear, grip the yoke itself with your left hand and pull the saw through the material (above). Return the saw to the rear of the guide fence before removing the material from the table top.

RIGHT- AND LEFT-HAND MITERS — METHOD No. 1. Since most mitering operations involve cutting both a right- and left-hand miter on the same piece of stock, it is possible to make both cuts with one setting of the saw. One method of doing this is to place a straight guide board at right angles to the guide fence. Use a try square to be sure the board is perpendicular to the guide fence and clamp the guide board to the table top. Be sure to leave space (at least the width of the board being cut) between the guide fence and guide board. With the machine in the right-hand miter position, place the stock to be cut against the guide board and butt the end against the guide fence. Cut the stock as previously described for right-hand miter cuts (top). When this cut is completed (it will be the left-hand miter cut), place the stock against the fence and make another right-hand miter cut on the other end as shown at the right.

RIGHT- AND LEFT-HAND MITERS — METHOD No. 2. The second method of making a right- and left-hand miter on the same piece of stock is with a V-board. With the saw in the standard crosscut position, place the edge of stock to be cut against the left side of the V-board and cut as shown in the illustration at the top left. This will give you the left-hand miter. Then, turn the stock around and make a cut with the stock against the right side of the V-board (bottom). When using this method, the stock must be cut to proper size before making the miters. Here, as in all other saw cuts, allow for the width of the kerf.

BEVEL MITERING. A bevel miter (sometimes called a compound or double miter) is a combination of a miter and a bevel. First set the saw to the angle desired by following the bevel scale; lock the bevel clamp handle. Then pull the arm clamp handle all the way forward, unlocking the arm and releasing the miter latch. Swing the radial arm into the desired miter position. Follow the same routine as for miter cuts. To make the cut, follow the normal operating routine described under bevel cross-cutting. Several uses are discussed later under compound angle cutting.

RIPPING. Straight ripping is done with the saw blade parallel to the guide fence and by feeding the material into the saw blade. You can rip from either the left or right side of the machine —the feeding of the material depends on the rotation of the saw blade. When ripping from the right side of the table (in-rip), the saw must be swiveled clockwise 90° from crosscut. If ripping from the left side of the machine (out-rip), swivel the saw counterclockwise 90° from the crosscut. But, before doing any ripping, the safety guard and anti-kickback must be adjusted to the proper position. Lay the material that is to be ripped on the table top close to the guard. Release the wing nut holding the guard to the motor and move the guard down until the spring clip touches the top surface of the board to be ripped. Tighten the wing nut. On the opposite end of the safety guard is the anti-kickback assembly. Release the thumbscrew holding it and adjust the rod down until the fingers are $\frac{1}{8}$ inch below the top surface of the board you are ripping. Tighten the thumbscrew. On top of the guard is the dust spout. Adjust it so the spout is turned toward the back of the machine and will carry the dust away from you. If desired, replace the standard fingers with a splitter and anti-kickback device such as shown at the bottom. The splitter separates the wood when ripping and prevents saw bind. The fingers are adjusted in the same way as the standard ones just described.

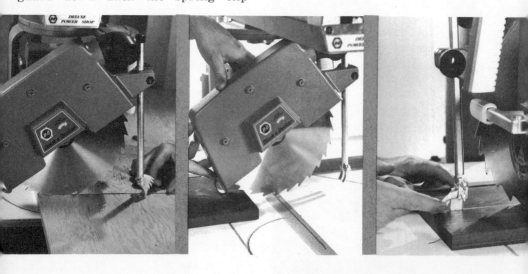

IN-RIP OPERATION. To set your saw at the in-rip position, pull the motor to the front of the radial arm. Release the yoke clamp handle by pulling it forward against the cam cup to release the locating pin. Swivel the yoke clockwise 90° from the crosscut position. (The yoke locating pin will snap into position automatically.) Now tighten the yoke clamp handle. The rip scale or rule on the right side of the arm is set with the guide fence in its standard position, which is between the stationary top and the spacer boards. With the saw blade against the guide fence, the pointer on the roller head should read zero on the *top* side of the ruler marked "in rip." With the saw set in the *in-rip* position, you *must feed the material into the saw from the right side of the machine.* With your left hand approximately 6 inches behind the safety guard, hold the material down and against the guide strip. With your right hand, move the material into the saw by standing on the right front side of the machine and let the material slide under your left hand. When your right hand is alongside your left hand, finish the rip by using an 18-inch pusher board. Hold the pusher board against the guide fence and against the end of the board you are ripping and continue pushing until the board you are ripping clears the opposite side of the saw blade by 2 inches. Pull the pusher board (two types are illustrated here) straight back. The type shown at the right should be used when the blade is close to the guide fence. In such cases the saw blade actually cuts into the pusher board.

OUT-RIP OPERATION. When ripping wide materials such as panel boards, you should swivel the saw 90° counterclockwise from the crosscut position to the out-rip position. With the saw set for out-ripping, follow the *lower* edge of the rip rule on the radial arm. This rule can be used to a capacity of 17½ inches with the guide fence in its standard position. If ripping wider material, it is necessary to move the guide fence to the rear of the table boards (left). Make the safety guard and anti-kickback adjustments as previously described. When the machine is set for *out-ripping, the material must be fed from the left side* (above right).

HORIZONTAL RIPPING. This is similar to horizontal crosscutting except that the cut is made on the side of the stock rather than on the end. To place the saw blade in the horizontal rip position, first set the saw in the in-rip position and tilt it to 90° as indicated on the bevel scale (follow the procedure described in horizontal crosscutting). Place the material to be cut against the regular or auxiliary table guide fence, depending on the material's thickness, and locate the height and depth of the cut. A piece of ¾-inch plywood can be used as an auxiliary table. Push it along with the stock when making the cut. The rip clamp is tightened and the material is pushed past the blade in the same manner as in straight ripping.

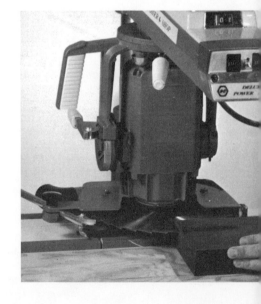

GROOVING. This is done in the same way as horizontal crosscutting or ripping. Place the saw in the crosscut or rip position, depending on the groove desired, and tilt it to the 90° bevel position. Set the blade (height and depth), place the material against the fence and push it past the blade, or pull the saw through the material if grooving the end of the stock. If the blade strikes the guide fence, place the stock on an auxiliary table. Raise or lower the arm a full turn on each pass of the saw blade and repeat the operation until the proper width is obtained. When an 8-inch blade is employed, be sure to use the special tool guard shown here.

RABBETING. This is merely cutting a groove along the edge of a board by taking two saw cuts at right angles to each other so as to remove a corner of the stock. It is used for picture, mirror, and window frames and for some furniture joints. Lay out the rabbet on the end of the board and mark it off. To make the first cut, place the material flat on the table top or on an auxiliary surface, against the fence, and make the cut with the saw in the horizontal rip position (below, left). The blade should be set at the desired rabbet depth and width. The second cut is made with the saw in the in-rip position and the blade set at a depth to make a clean corner (below). The rabbet can also be made by placing the saw in a horizontal rip position and making the first cut at the top edge of the board. Then lower the blade a full turn at a time until the desired depth of the rabbet is reached.

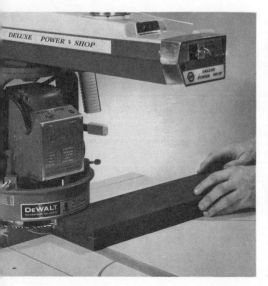

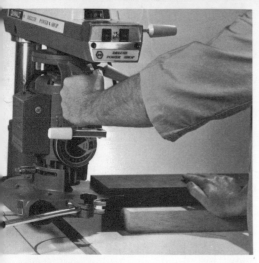 

END RABBET. To make an end rabbet, lay the material flat against the fence and make the first cut along the end with the saw in the horizontal position (above). Make the second cut to the depth of the rabbet with the saw in the standard crosscut position (above right). A rabbet can also be cut in the same manner as a groove.

With the saw in the horizontal position, set the depth of the rabbet and start cutting at the top edge of the board. Lower the blade a full turn at a time until the desired rabbet is obtained. Rabbets can be cut with only one pass by using the dado head (page 46).

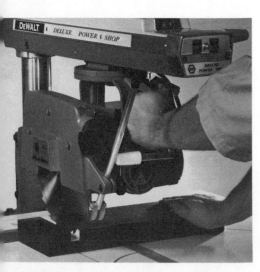 

DADO CUTTING. A dado is a groove cut across the grain. With the saw in the crosscut position, lower the blade to the desired depth of the dado. Start at one end of the dado and pull the saw through the material. After returning the saw to the column, shift the material ⅛ inch and bring the saw forward again. Continue until the desired width of the dado is obtained. Dadoes can be made with one cut by using the dado head (page 43).

PLOUGHING. By placing the saw in the in-rip position and using the dadoing technique, you can plough a groove in a board. Lower the blade to the desired depth and set it at one end of the cut. Then push the material past the blade as in ripping. Move the blade ⅛ inch on the rip scale toward the other end of the cut and push the material past the blade again. Continue until the desired width is obtained.

BEVEL RIPPING. This operation is simply ripping with the saw tilted for angle cuts. With the saw in the rip position (either in- or out-rip), elevate the column by rotating the handle, release the bevel clamp handle and locating pin. Tilt the motor to the desired angle. If the 45° position is wanted, the bevel locating pin will quickly locate it. For any desired angle, use the bevel scale and securely lock the motor in place with the bevel clamp handle. Adjust the guard on the in-feed end so the spring clip is about ⅛ inch above the surface and the anti-kickback should be adjusted as illustrated above. Use a flat pusher board as previously described. Push material until it clears the saw on opposite side of blade.

V-CUTTING. As you'll see in succeeding chapters, one of the most useful jigs you can make is a V-block. It can be made easily by bevel-ripping. After placing the blade in the 45° position, lower the blade to the desired depth of the V. Locate the blade's position on the rip scale and lock the rip clamp. Start the motor and move the stock past the blade as previously described. Turn the stock around and pass it through the saw again.

BEVEL RABBET. This cut is made in the same manner as a standard rabbet except that both cuts are made at an angle as illustrated above.

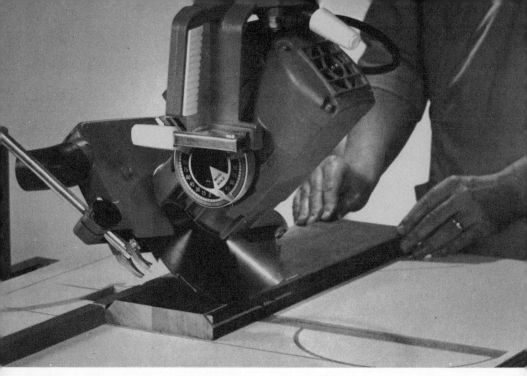

CHAMFER CUTTING. A chamfer is simply a bevel cut along the top edges of stock. Set the saw in the bevel-rip position at the desired angle. Position the blade so it overhangs the stock by the desired width of the cut and lock it in place with the rip clamp. Push the stock along the guide fence and through the blade. Reverse the material and cut along the other top edge in the same manner. Cross-chamfering is done by placing the blade at the desired angle in the bevel-crosscut position. Position the blade so it overhangs the stock by the desired width (as in rip-chamfering). Then pull the saw through in the prescribed crosscut method. The octagon shape required for spindle lathe work can be cut in the same way as a rip-chamfer.

RAISED-PANEL CUTTING. This operation can add immeasurably to the beauty of a finished-door project. Actually, raised-panel cutting is simply bevel-ripping. Use an 8-inch diameter blade in place of the standard 10-inch blade since the latter may strike the column base. Place the saw in the out-rip position and tilt it to the 90° bevel position. Then raise it 5° to 10° (indicated as 80° to 85° on the bevel scale). Position the blade so it overhangs the guide fence (either on the stationary or auxiliary table, depending on the thickness of the material) by the desired width of the cut. To do this, move the saw the desired distance from the column and lock it in position with the rip clamp. Before starting the motor, be sure the saw blade moves freely. Then push the stock along the guide fence, feeding from right to left. Cut end grain portion first. For this operation, it's wise to use the special tool guard.

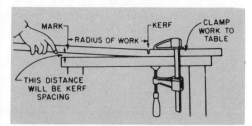

MARK — RADIUS OF WORK — KERF — CLAMP WORK TO TABLE

THIS DISTANCE WILL BE KERF SPACING

KERFING

KERFING. It is often necessary to bend wood. When the problem of curved surfaces arises, you have a choice of three methods: (1) bending the wood by steaming it (this calls for special equipment), (2) building the curve up by sawing thick segments of the circle on a saber saw (which means that a great deal of expensive wood would be wasted), or (3) cutting a series of saw kerfs to within $1/16$ inch of the outside surface to make the material more flexible for bending. The third is the most practical method and is used to round off the corners of paneled walls, shape aprons for counters and hollow cores for drum tables, form contoured chair seats and backs, bend trellis tops, and make curved forms for poured concrete. The idea is to make a number of deep side-by-side cuts in the face of the stock. These will form the underside of the bend. This turns the opposite face into a flexible veneer. Naturally, the distance between the saw kerfs determines the flexibility of the stock and the radius to which it can be bent. In order to form a more rigid curve, the saw kerfs should be as close together as possible. To determine the proper spacing, first decide on the radius of the curve or circle to be formed. After the radius has been determined, measure this same distance (the radius) from the end of the stock as shown here and make a saw kerf at this point. The kerf can be made in the crosscut position with the blade lowered to $1/16$-inch above the bottom of the stock. Fasten the stock to the table top with a C clamp. Raise the end of the stock until the saw kerf is closed, as shown above. The distance the end of the stock is raised above the table in order to close the kerf determines the distance needed between saw kerfs.

CUTTING KERFS. Since most bending operations require many saw kerfs, mark the spacing on the guide fence with a pencil. Cut the first kerf where you wish to start the bend. Measure and mark material for second kerf and make cut. Without moving stock place a mark on guide fence at first kerf. The remaining cuts are located by placing each new kerf at the guide fence mark and making the new cut (below). Cutting kerfs at an angle (center) produces a spiral curve like that shown at the bottom. In either case, when the kerfing is complete, the stock is slowly bent until it matches the required curve. Wetting the wood with warm water will aid the bending process, while a tie strip tacked in place will hold the shape until the part is attached to the assembly. Even compound curves may be formed in this manner by kerfing both sides of the work. When kerfing is exposed, veneers can be glued in place to hide the cuts. When bending wood for exterior work, the kerfs should be coated with glue before the piece is shaped. After bending, wood plastic and putty may be used to fill the crevices. When finished properly, only close examination will reveal the method used to make the bend.

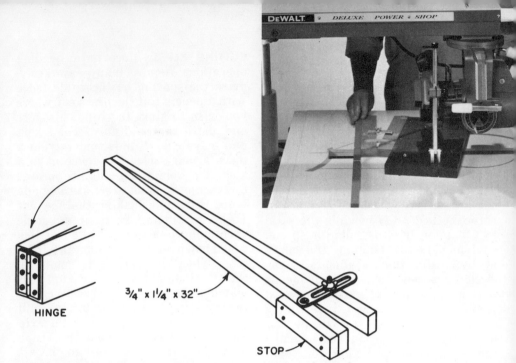

³/₄" x 1¹/₄" x 32"

HINGE

STOP

TAPER RIPPING—METHOD No. 1. Taper ripping is generally used to construct tapered furniture legs. One of the several jigs shown here may be used. But before using a jig, all edges to be tapered should be squared if uniform sides are desired. One such jig is shown above. When hinging the ends, keep the two pieces clamped together. The crosspiece or brace which secures the setting can be made of metal or hardwood. When the jig is complete, mark a line across both pieces 12 inches from the hinged end. Set the jig by measuring between these two marks to determine the taper per foot. The formula used for a so-called two-sided taper (actually, all four sides are tapered) is

Taper per foot =
$$\frac{W \text{ (top width)} - w \text{ (bottom width)}}{L \text{ (length of taper)}} \times 6$$

For example, if you are making a coffee-table leg 18 inches long, 5 inches wide at the top, and 3½ inches wide at the bottom, you would require a ½-inch taper per foot.

Taper per foot =
$$\frac{5 - 3.5}{18} \times \frac{6}{1} = \frac{1.5}{3} = 0.5 \text{ or } ½ \text{ inch per foot}$$

By opening the jig ½ inch at the 1-foot mark, you have the proper setting. For a so-called one-side taper (two sides are tapered) use the following formula:

Taper per foot =
$$\frac{W \text{ (top width)} - w \text{ (bottom width)}}{L \text{ (Length of taper)}} \times 12$$

Using these dimensions, you would find the one-side taper as follows:

Taper per foot =
$$\frac{5 - 3.5}{18} \times \frac{12}{1} = \frac{3}{3} = 1 \text{ inch}$$

To use the jig, place the flat side against the fence and the material to be tapered in the stop at the end of the jig. With the saw in the rip position, push the jig past the blade as if it were a normal ripping operation (above). Continue the ripping operation on all four sides in the same manner. When the project calls for a two-side taper, double the jig setting for the second pass. Be sure the first tapered side of the work is placed against the jig when making the second pass. Square legs with a taper on each face are made by setting the location of the saw blade to equal the combined width of the jig and the work. Make one pass; then make the second pass on the adjacent face. Open the jig to twice the original setting and adjust the blade so the wide end of the work just touches it. Make the third pass on the next adjacent face and then make the fourth and final pass.

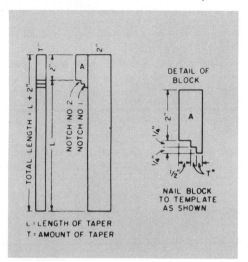

TOTAL LENGTH = L + 2"
L = LENGTH OF TAPER
T = AMOUNT OF TAPER

NOTCH NO 2
NOTCH NO 1

DETAIL OF BLOCK

NAIL BLOCK TO TEMPLATE AS SHOWN

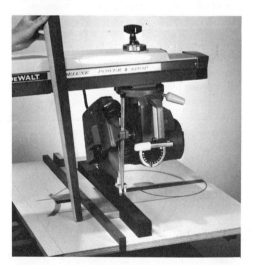

TAPER RIPPING—METHOD No. 2. The step jig shown at the left is good for production work because it eliminates setting the variable jig for different tapers. The steps gauge the taper and are dimensioned for the various tapers needed. One corner of the work is placed in the correct step while the other end rides against the arm of the jig. The material is placed in the first notch of the jig, and the combined jig and work are pushed into the saw in a rip position (above). An adjacent side of the work is cut in the same manner. The two remaining sides are cut with the work in the second notch (left).

TAPER RIPPING—METHOD No. 3. Tapering with a radial-arm machine can be done without the use of any jigs whatsoever. In the so-called "floating blade" method, the saw is placed in the in-rip position. The radial arm is then set to the left a given number of degrees. (One degree offset to the left will give approximately a 1/4-inch per foot taper. As shown here, the arm is set at 4° and thus the taper would be approximately 1–inch taper per foot.) The rip clamp must *not* be locked and the anti-kickback fingers should *not* touch the board. As the board is pushed past the saw blade, the desired taper will result.

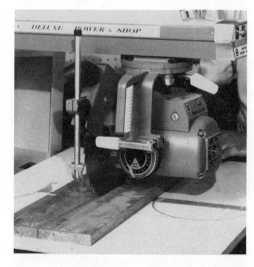

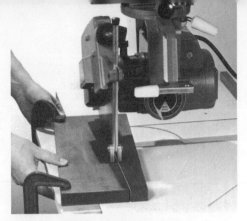

front edge of the table top becomes a second "guide fence." You can taper rip at any predetermined angle with this method. Just decide the degree of taper desired; then clamp on the lower guide board accordingly. As shown, the saw is placed in the out-rip position for this taper-rip operation. This allows the blade to be positioned directly above the front edge of the worktable. Thus, the completed cut corresponds exactly to the angle at which the guide board is clamped to the stock.

TAPER RIPPING—METHOD No. 4. Taper ripping can also be accomplished by simply clamping a piece of narrow stock to the lower edge of the material to be ripped. In this way, the

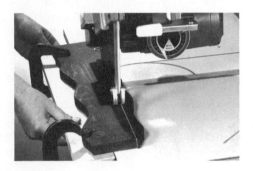

RIPPING IRREGULAR SHAPES. Method number four of taper cutting can also be used for straightening the irregular edges of lumber. A straight-edge is clamped to the work and is pushed past the saw blade, with the straight-edge riding against the front edge of the saw table. The resulting cut will be parallel to the straightedge.

SAW MOLDINGS. Several attractive moldings can be made with cuts similar to those for kerfing. The design shown below is commonly called a dentil molding, although this term has a broad application and can include many different shapes. A spacer mark on the guide fence, as for kerfing, should be used. The saw is set in the crosscut position, and the blade is lowered to the depth desired. Repeat cuts are made by alternating work faces. The molding is then made by ripping narrow strips from the work. Ripping on work as narrow and delicate as this demands care and accuracy. Use a pusher to push the molding past the blade. Molding should be cut with a planer or plywood blade to assure clean cutting. After the dentil molding is cut, it can be used as an overlay, or the molding can be applied to a heavier backing piece of contrasting color.

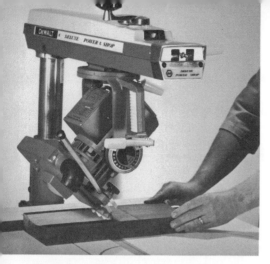
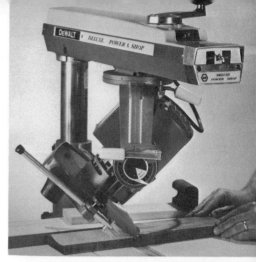

CONTOUR CUTTING. One of the most novel techniques in radial-arm saw operations is the contour feed for cutting coves. On the standard circular saw this is a fairly difficult task; but on the radial-arm saw it is quite simple. Place the material flat on the table top against the guide fence. Set the saw at a 45° bevel position. Locate the motor so the lowest point of the blade is on the center line of the material and tighten the rip clamp. Remove the material from near the saw and lower the blade so it is not more than 1/8 inch below the top surface of the stock. Turn on the machine and push the material past the saw blade as in ripping (above). Continue this procedure, lowering the blade one full turn (1/8 inch) at a time, until the de-sired depth of the cut is obtained. The final cut should be a light one for a smooth finish. The saw cut can be made in different angle positions for different effects. For instance, you may set the bevel at 45° and turn the yoke off center. This will change the radius of the cut. Experiment with scrap wood until you get the effect you desire. A half-circle effect, suitable for modern picture frames, is cut by establishing the depth of cut at the edge of the material and pushing the material past the blade in the same manner as just described (above). While a saw blade does a good job on contour cutting if care is exercised, best results can be had with a dado head (see page 50).

SAUCER CUTTING. This cut makes intricate decorative patterns easily. Remove the guide fence and the back table boards and clamp the stock as shown. Elevate the column, then tilt the motor to a 45° bevel. Locate the blade over the center line of the stock. Tighten the rip clamp. Turn on the machine and lower the motor until the blade strikes the stock. With your left hand on the anti-kickback rod, pull out the bevel clamp handle, unlocking the clamp and releasing the locating pin. Then swing the blade in an arc past the stock and back to the vertical position. Lower the saw blade one-half turn of the elevating handle and continue the cutting process until the desired depth is reached.

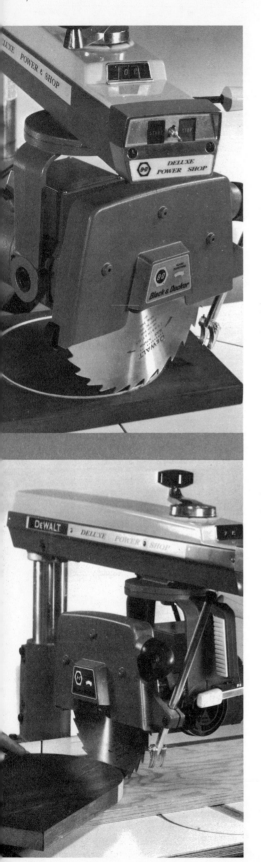

CIRCLE CUTTING. There are two basic ways to cut circles with a radial-arm machine. In the first, shown at the top, the stock is clamped to the table so its center is directly in line with the center of the arm. The motor is also located over the center of the stock and the rip clamp is locked in place. Then lower the saw blade until it touches the material. With the saw turned on, lower the blade by turning the elevating handle one full turn. Put your left hand on the yoke handle. With your right hand, pull the yoke clamp handle all the way forward, releasing the locating pin. Swing the motor in a counterclockwise, then clockwise direction to complete a 360° turn. Lower the saw blade one half turn of the elevating handle and continue this process until the circle has been cut. It's a good idea when using this technique to do the cutting on a plywood or hardboard auxiliary table. Circles from ½ to 10 inches can be made by beveling the saw blade. For example: With the 10-inch saw blade set at 0° on the bevel scale, you will cut a 9-inch circle; at 5° left bevel (left of 0 on bevel scale), a 10-inch diameter circle will result: and at 30° right bevel, the circle will be 2⅞ inches in diameter. The technique shown at the bottom can be used to make any size circles. A simple jig fixture is necessary. It consists of a ¾-inch-thick board with an inverted fence nailed to one edge. The inverted fence is clamped in place of the regular guide fence. This holds the jig. A nail, with the head cut off, is driven into the ¾-inch board at the proper location. Then the stock to be cut is pressed onto the nail and pivoted as a series of crosscuts are made.

COMPOUND ANGLE CUTTING. Compound angle cutting on the radial-arm machine is a simple operation. A compound angle is merely a miter and bevel cut made at the same time. Any frame or open structure with sloping sides, Jack rafter, hip-roof rafter, or shadow-box picture frame is made with a compound angle cut. A knowledge of geometry is not necessary to make this cut if the chart shown here is used. All you must decide is the angle of slant or the pitch of the sides. Suppose, for example, you are making a four-sided shadow-box picture frame with the sides sloping out at 45°. This would mean your pitch is 45°. Simply go to the curved line on the chart labeled square box and find the 45° mark. Follow the horizontal line, intersecting the curved line at 45°, to the left. It reads 35°. This is your miter setting. Then follow the vertical line intersecting at 45° down to the bottom of the chart. It reads 30°. This is your bevel setting. With the machine set at these two positions all you need do now is make the cut. When all four sides are cut to length you will have a four-sided shadow-box frame. For six or eight sided boxes use the corresponding curve and follow the same procedure.

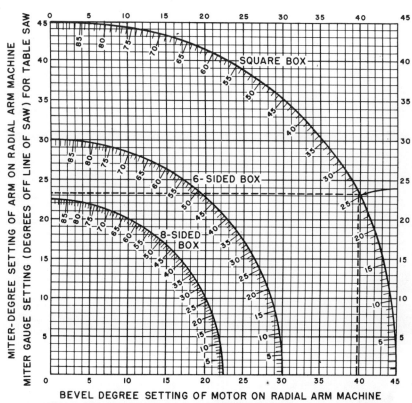

MITER-DEGREE SETTING OF ARM ON RADIAL ARM MACHINE

MITER GAUGE SETTING (DEGREES OFF LINE OF SAW) FOR TABLE SAW

SQUARE BOX

6-SIDED BOX

8-SIDED BOX

BEVEL DEGREE SETTING OF MOTOR ON RADIAL ARM MACHINE
TABLE OR BLADE SETTING (DEGREES OFF VERTICAL) FOR TABLE SAW

ROSETTE CUTTING. Diamond shapes involve another type of compound-angle cutting. After bevel ripping the stock into V–strips, set the motor at the 45° right-hand miter position and the 45° bevel position. Make the first cut with the V–strip to the left of the blade. For the second cut place the strip to the right of the blade as illustrated.

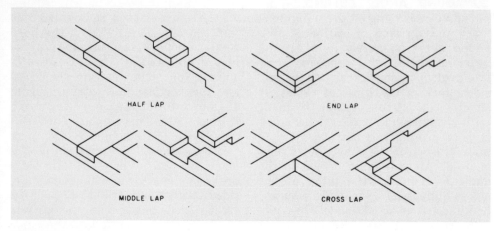

HALF LAP

END LAP

MIDDLE LAP

CROSS LAP

LAP-JOINT CUTTING. There are several types of lapped or halved joints. To make the end lap, place the motor in the vertical position (the horizontal crosscut sawing position) and install an auxiliary table in place of the standard guide fence. Both pieces of stock that are to form the joint can be cut at once—laid side by side on the auxiliary table. Make the first cut with the blade passing through the center of the stock, following the technique described for horizontal crosscutting. Elevate the blade ⅛ inch (the width of the blade) by turning the elevating handle one full turn for each successive cut until all excess stock has been removed. The other types of lap joints shown above are combinations of end lap joints and dado cuts. Production work makes use of the dado head in order to reduce the number of passes needed.

LOCK JOINT CUTTING. To make this joint first it is necessary to find the exact thickness of your saw blade. To do this, place a piece of scrap wood on the auxiliary table illustrated here and make a cut flush with the bottom edge. Now elevate the machine one turn (⅛ inch) and make a second cut. Elevate again and make a third cut. You have now made three cuts with two tongues left standing. Break off the bottom tongue and fit it into the top sawcut. If it fits too loosely, elevate the machine slightly more than one turn before each cut. This is a trial and error situation. Once you have found the correct elevation for spacing you can complete the joint fairly quickly on good lumber. It is best to use a planer or plywood blade for this joint.

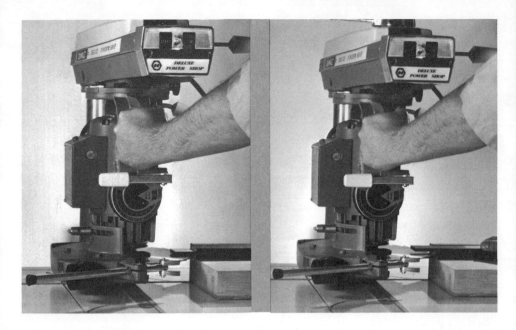

TENON AND MORTISE CUTTING. The tenon is made in the same manner as the lap joint except the stock left standing is in the middle rather than on one side of the material (above). The full tenon, when combined with a tight-fitting mortise and properly glued or doweled, gives a very strong joint which is widely used in all phases of cabinetmaking and general woodworking. The mortise is the other half of the joint into which the tenon fits. Making the mortise consists simply of cutting a groove the same width as the previously made tenon (above right).

DOVETAIL TAPER. Wide pieces of solid lumber are often fitted with dovetail keys to prevent warping. To do this, you'll need some taper—it may vary from ⅛– to ⅜–inch per foot—since it is almost impossible to drive a straight key for any distance. To make the cut, set the saw in the in-rip position and bevel the blade 10° toward the outboard position. Using the tapering jig described on page 32, which has been set to cut the desired taper, the work and jig are advanced into the saw along the guide fence. By making a series of successive cuts in both the out-rip and in-rip positions, the angled side of the dovetail is made. The keys can be cut without any changes in the blade tilt, using the jig at the setting previously set for the angled side. The keys should be made a little longer than necessary, cutting off flush after the key has been inserted.

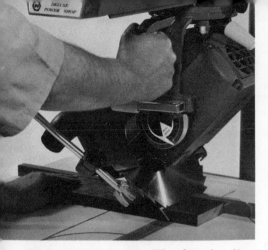

BEVEL-SPLINE JOINT. The bevel-spline joint is made by bevel crosscutting the ends of the stock with the motor locked in the 45° bevel position. To make the slot for the spline, reverse the stock on the table and, with the motor still in the bevel position (but elevated to the proper height, approx-imately $\frac{3}{8}$ inch, so the blade will not cut completely through), pull the saw across the previously made bevel crosscut, leaving the shallow slot. Make the spline itself from any $\frac{1}{8}$-inch rippings you may have—simply cut to the desired size to fit the spline joint.

RESAWING. If extremely thick wood is being ripped into thinner boards, it is often necessary to cut partially through the board, invert the board, and complete the cut. This operation is generally called resawing. When resawing, the blade should be placed in the in-rip position. The blade should be set just a little over half the width of the board when the board is less in width than twice the capacity of the saw. To illustrate this, let us assume that it is necessary to resaw a board 4 inches wide by $\frac{7}{8}$ inches thick into two boards 4 by $\frac{3}{8}$ inches. Making an allowance of $\frac{1}{8}$ inch for the kerf or the waste material by the blade, and taking into consideration that the capacity of the particular saw blade is 3 inches, about 1 inch is left for the second cut. However, when the width of the board to be resawed is greater than twice the capacity of the machine, make the cuts as deep as possible from each edge. Then finish the rip-ping by hand. When resawing 4-inch stock and larger, use a guide fence approximately $3\frac{1}{2}$ inches high. An important point to remember always when resawing is to keep the same surface of the board against the guide fence for both cuts—reverse the board end for end, never side for side. When resawing be sure to follow all the safety rules for straight ripping.

CHAPTER 3

DADOING

Without a doubt the first accessory you'll want for your radial-arm machine is a dado head. This important addition to the home workshop contains a series of saw blades and chippers which can cut grooves, rabbets, mortises, tenons, etc., in thicknesses from $\frac{1}{8}$ to $^{13}/_{16}$ inch in a single pass. In other words, the dado head cuts down the time consumed in making many wood joints.

There are basically two types of dado heads; the flat–ground and the hollow–ground. While the latter is more expensive, it produces a much smoother cut and should be used in high-quality work. Either type consists of two outside saws, each about $\frac{1}{8}$ inch thick, whose teeth are not given any set, and inside saws, or "chippers" one $\frac{1}{4}$-inch, two $\frac{1}{8}$-inch (some heads include two additional $\frac{1}{8}$-inch chippers instead of the $\frac{1}{4}$-inch one), and one $^{1}/_{16}$-inch thick (thickness at the hub). The cutting portions of the chippers are wider than the hub to overlap the adjacent cutter or saw. When assembling a cutter head, arrange the two outside saws so that the large raker teeth on one are opposite the small cutting teeth on the other. This produces a smoother cutting and easier running head. Also, be sure the wide cutting portion of the chippers are placed in the gullets of the outside saws, not against the teeth, so that the head cuts clean and chips have room to

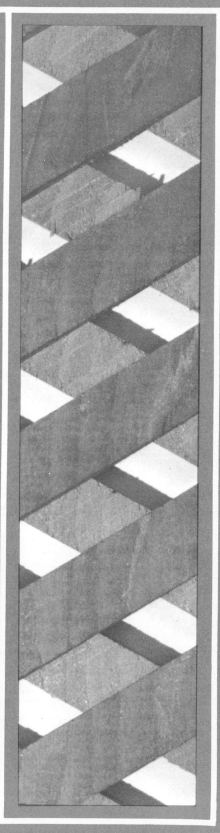

come out. Stagger the inside cutters so their teeth do not come together. For example, if three cutters are used, they should be set 60° apart.

Never use the chipper blades without the two outside saws. For example, to cut a dado $\frac{1}{2}$-inch wide, use the two outside saws, each $\frac{1}{8}$-inch in width, plus a single $\frac{1}{4}$-inch or two $\frac{1}{8}$-inch chippers. Actually, any width dado head can be used—the size is limited only by the length of the motor arbor. However, most dado-head sets have only enough blades to make cuts up to $^{13}/_{16}$ inch wide.

When the width of the finished cut is to be wider than the dado head, make two successive cuts. If more than one cut is required they must overlap a bit at the center. If the width of the dado is more than twice the capacity of the cutter head, set the head for slightly over one-third of the dado width and make three overlapping cuts. If needed, you can control the exact width of the groove with paper washers. These washers, 3 to 4 inches in diameter, can be placed between the blades and chippers. You can increase the width even more with cardboard (up to $^{1}/_{16}$-inch thick) instead of paper.

The design of the dado head's cutting teeth permits sawing with the grain, across the grain, or at an angle.

TIPS ON DADO-HEAD USE

- Don't use a dull dado—sharpen it.
- Assemble chippers and outside blades so none of the teeth are in line with each other. Teeth lined up like marching soldiers produce a noisy cut. Staggered teeth smooth the cutting action.
- Make cuts slowly and smoothly. Don't cut too deep. If excessively deep cuts are required, make them in multiple passes with your dado blade.
- If you can't do a good sharpening job yourself (and most of us can't), go to a professional.
- Keep your dado parts clean. Check them periodically and, if necessary, clean away gum and dirt deposits with a cloth dipped in turpentine or lighter fluid. Store the parts carefully. Don't let cutting edges knock against other surfaces. If storing parts, especially outside blades, for any length of time, protect them with a light film of oil.

MOUNTING THE DADO HEAD. The dado head is installed on the motor shaft in the same manner as the saw blade (page 16). For dado cuts up to $\frac{1}{2}$ inch in width, first place one of the arbor collars on the shaft, with its recessed side toward the end of the shaft; the dado-head assembly next; then the other arbor collar, with its recessed side against the dado head; finally, tighten the arbor nut with both the Allen and hex wrenches. For cuts over $\frac{1}{2}$ inch, omit the second arbor collar. When using the full dado, use the inside collar, the 13/16-inch dado, and the arbor nut. Regardless of the thickness of the dado cut employed, mount the safety guard over the blades and tighten the wing nut.

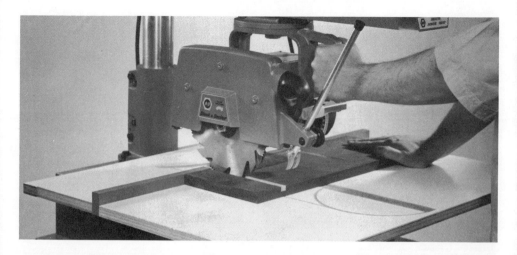

PLAIN DADO. A cross dado is a groove cut across the grain. It is done the same way as crosscutting. With the motor in the crosscut position, adjust the radial arm until the depth of the groove is obtained. Then pull the motor past the stock, which has been placed tight against the guide fence. To locate the dado, lay the second member over the piece to be cut and mark the desired width. Draw a line across either edge and mark the depth of the dado—usually half the thickness of the stock. You can predetermine the depth of the cut by lowering the dado until it barely touches the top of the stock, and then lowering the arm one full turn for each $\frac{1}{8}$ inch of desired depth. When more than one piece is to be grooved, the *stop block* arrangement described on page 18 can be used to good advantage.

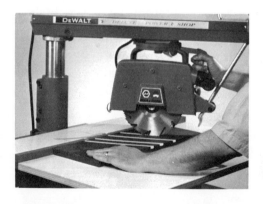

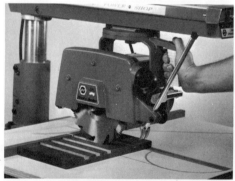

ANGLE DADO. This cut has many uses in cabinetmaking, construction work, and general woodworking. Among other applications, the angle-dado cut is used to recess treads in stair construction, in joining the sill to the upright members of a window frame, and to recess the narrow strips in shutters, louvers, etc. This cut is made in the same manner as the cross dado, except that the radial arm is moved to the desired degree of angle as indicated on the miter scale.

PARALLEL DADOES. These are a series of dado cuts—either cross or angle— exactly parallel to one another. With the radial-arm machine, these cuts are easy to make because the material is moved to a mark or stop on the guide fence for each suceeding cut. As a result, two cuts made with the radial-arm in the same position are always parallel. The material is held with the left hand against the guide fence.

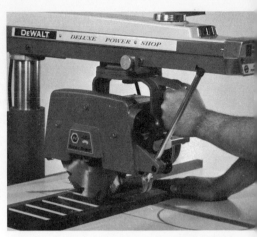

BLIND DADO. A blind dado, or gain, goes only partly across the board. With the stock against the guide fence, mark where you wish the dado to stop. Then place a stop clamp on the machine as shown at the left.

With the dado head in the crosscut position, lower it to the desired depth and pull forward to the stop. If a square cut at the blind end of the dado is desired, it can be made with a wood chisel.

CORNER DADO. To make a corner-dado cut, place the stock at 45° in a V-block and clamp the block to the guide fence. Raise or lower the arm until the proper depth is obtained. Pull the motor through the stock in the standard crosscut procedure. The stock can project beyond the block, or the block may be partially cut away to permit the passage of the dado head.

PLOUGHING. The ploughing operation with a dado head corresponds to the rip cut with a saw blade. Set the radial arm at 0° (crosscut position) ; swivel the yoke 90° from the crosscut position ; move the carriage along the arm to the desired width and lock ; raise or lower the column to the desired groove depth. Adjust the safety guard so the spring clip on the in-feed touches the stock, lock the wing nut, and lower the anti-kickback fingers 1/8 inch below the surface of the board. Push the material against the guide fence past the blade. Always feed material *into* rotation of the blade—never from anti-kickback end of guard.

BLIND PLOUGHING. Center or blind ploughing is done with the motor in the rip position. Elevate the dado head, place the work beneath the blade at the point where the cut is to be made, start the machine, and lower the blade to the desired depth of cut. Hold the material firmly and push through the dado as in ripping. When the cut is completed, raise the arm so the lumber can be pulled from beneath the cutting tool. Blind grooves are usually cut to marks; however, stop block can be used when several pieces are to be ploughed to the same length.

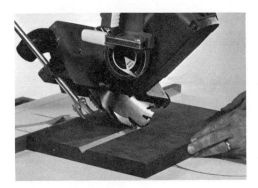

BEVEL PLOUGHING. This operation leaves a smooth, accurate V-groove in the stock. It has many applications, both functional and decorative, in cabinetmaking and general woodworking. It also can be used to make V-block jigs. Bevel ploughing is done with the radial arm and yoke positioned as for straight ploughing. In this operation, however, the motor is tilted to the 45° position. To tilt the motor, release the bevel clamp and the bevel latch, tilt the motor, and then reset these controls. The bevel latch locates the 45° angle automatically. (Other angles can be used and are located on the protractor scale and held in place with the bevel clamp.) With the material against the fence, move the motor to the desired width and lock the rip clamp. Raise or lower the arm to the desired depth for the V and push the stock past the dado head in the usual rip manner.

FLUTING. This consists of making a series of parallel V-grooves. Fluting is done with the motor in the bevel-plough position. With many conventional-type woodworking machines, it is a real problem to get the grooves an equal distance apart. This problem is eliminated with a radial-arm machine because the rip scale allows you to position the motor accurately, and the rigid, square guide fence ensures that cuts will be parallel. The elevating handle controls the depth of the cut, and the material is pushed past the cutter as in all other ploughing operations. The finished cuts can be used to simulate pillars or columns in cupboards or fireplace mantels.

MOUNTING SPECIAL TOOL GUARD.
Anytime the dado-head blades are used in a horizontal position, the special tool should be used in place of the regular guard. After the dado head has been installed, place the tool guard on the motor in exactly the same way as you mount the saw guard and lock it in place with the wing nut. To allow the guard to be raised high enough for the operator to check the position of the cutting tool, two thumbscrews, located on either side of the center nut, permit the protecting portion of the guard to be freely raised and lowered on the small circular columns. When raised, and locked in position by retightening the thumbscrews, the guard permits full access to the blades.

RABBETING. Grooving a notch from the side and top of the lumber is easy with the radial-arm machine. Elevate the arm until you have sufficient space beneath the motor to allow the cutting tool to swing to a horizontal setting. Release the bevel clamp handle and the bevel locating pin and put the dado head in the horizontal position. (Anytime the dado-head blades are used in a horizontal position be sure that the tool guard is installed.) To set the width of the rabbet, use the rip scale located on the radial arm. Lower the arm to the desired depth and move the material past the cutters from the right side of the table. Again, it is important to remember always to feed into the rotation of the tool. If thin stock is to be rabbeted, use the auxiliary table top shown on page 26 and set it in place of the standard guide fence. To lay out a rabbet joint, hold the piece to be fitted into the rabbet on the stock to be rabbeted and mark the width of the cut.

BEVEL RABBETING. The bevel rabbet is made in a manner similar to the straight rabbet except that the motor is placed at some angle less than 90° (vertical position), depending upon the degree of bevel desired. This cut is widely employed in construction, cabinetmaking, and general-millwork operations.

CUTTING AND DADOING. It is possible, by combining a saw blade and the dado head, to get both a cutoff and dado at the same time. Install the saw blade first on the arbor, followed by the dado head. Then, with the saw in the crosscut position, pull the yoke through the material (top). Result —cutoff and dado in the same action. The diameter of the saw blade and dado depends on the lumber's thickness and the depth of dado. Use a 10-inch saw blade and an 8-inch-diameter dado head, as a rule, for most cuts. It is also possible to rip and plough at the same time. Mount the saw blade and dado head on the arbor and put the motor in the rip position. Lower the column to the desired depth and push the stock past the blade and dado head (bottom).

GROOVING. Although the term "groove" is used to denote many types of dado cuts, it is usually applied to the dado operation made on the side, as opposed to the top or end, surface of stock. The operation is exactly the same as for rabbeting except that the arm is lowered so the cutting head is below the top surface of the lumber. Thus, the finished cut is bound on two sides by remaining stock, instead of only one as in the rabbet cut. (Note the use of the ¼-inch plywood as an auxiliary table to clear the guide fence.) Using the dado head gives you an extra-wide groove, eliminating a number of passes that are necessary when grooving with a saw blade.

BLIND GROOVING. Blind mortising or blind grooving is the same as grooving except that the cut is not carried completely through the stock. In many cases, where the ends of the lumber will be exposed, it is not desirable to show the side groove. In such cases, the stock is pivoted into the cutting head at the desired distance from the end. As a rule stop blocks are used to locate the beginning and end of the blind groove. Long cuts of this kind are commonly employed in making spline butt joints.

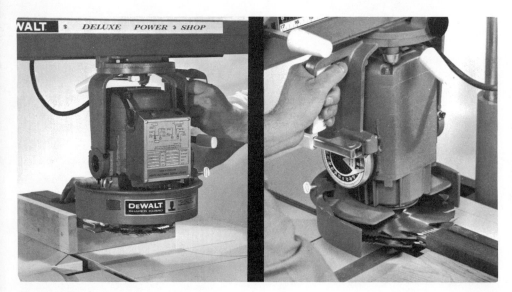

TENONING. To cut the stock for a mortise and tenon joint, the motor is placed in the vertical position with the dado head in the horizontal position. A spacing collar is inserted into the dado head at the proper place so the stock forming the tenon is left standing. Using an auxiliary table, place the material against the fence and mark the stock for the desired tongue or groove depth. The dado head should be located at the proper height, and the motor brought forward to cut the tenon. You can make either a single tenon or double tenon by the placing of the spacer collar and saw position.

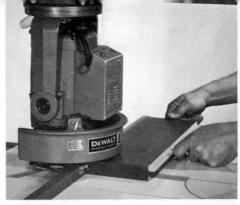

MORTISING. This operation is actually the reverse of the one used for tenons. Making the mortise consists simply of cutting a groove to the same width as a previously made single tenon. Be sure the lengths of the tenon and mortise are the same. Various types of mortise and tenon joints are shown on page 123.

TONGUE AND GROOVE. You can make your own flooring, wood panels, etc. with this cut. The tongue and groove is a combination of tenon and grooving previously described. With the saw in the horizontal rip position, cut the tongue to the exact dimension needed using the dado inserts with collars. Push the stock past the blade to complete the tongue. Cut all the tongues on the required panels first; then turn the stock over and cut the grooves as shown above.

CUTTING LAP JOINTS. The joints illustrated on page 38 are very easy to cut with the dado head. To lay out a *cross-lap* joint (left), mark a line across the surface of one member to indicate one side of the dado. Place the second member over it and mark the width. Invert the pieces and mark the width on the second member. Draw lines along the edges of both pieces and mark the depth of the dado, which should be one-half the thickness of the piece. The *edge-lap* joint is identical except that the members cross on edge. The *middle- or tee-lap* joint (right) is made with one member exactly like the cross-lap joint

(left) and the second member cut on the end (right). The *end-lap* joint, which is used in frame construction, is made by laying out and cutting *both* pieces as shown at right. The *half-lap* joint is cut in the same way except that the pieces are joined end to end. The *end-lap* and *half-lap* joints are actually two tenons with the stock removed from only one side. With the motor in the vertical position, lay the stock, side by side, against the guide fence on the auxiliary table. Raise or lower the radial arm until the lower blade is in the middle of the stock, and then pull the cutter through as in the ordinary crosscutting procedure.

SCALLOPING. For window valances, scallop cutting is ideal. Place the dado head in the horizontal ripping position. Locate the motor on the radial arm so the dado head overhangs the guide fence, and lock it in place after determining the width of the cut desired. Then, lower the column to position the blade to the desired depth of the cut. Start the machine and feed the stock into the dado by heeling or pivoting it on the right side of the guide fence as shown. The design may be varied by changing the overhang of the dado head.

PANEL SINKING. This decorative door pattern is a combination of cross dadoing and ploughing. Mark the layout of the design and locate the motor above the beginning of the first cross-dado cut. Turn the machine on and lower the blade until it is $1/8$ inch below the surface of the panel. Then pull the yoke to the end of the marked design (top) and elevate the motor. Repeat the cut at the other end. Now swing the motor to the in-rip position and lower the arm into the beginning of the cross-dado cut. Push the material past the dado until it reaches the other cross-dado cut (bottom). Elevate the motor and cut the final side of the design in the same manner. Use a wood chisel to square the corners if you wish.

RADIUS CUTTING. This is a dado operation used to produce a concave cut along the face of a piece of lumber. It is accomplished by elevating the column (the radial arm and yoke remain in the normal crosscut position) and tilting the motor to the 45° bevel position. The motor is moved in or out on the radial arm to the correct position in relation to the stock and is locked in place. The lumber is pushed under the cutting head as when ripping or ploughing. The first cut should be about $1/8$ inch and the dado head should be lowered one full turn at a time until the desired concave is obtained. This operation is similar to contour cutting with a saw blade (page 35) and the various cuts described can be made in the same manner when using a dado head. Actually, contour and radius cutting is more suited to the dado attachment than the saw blade.

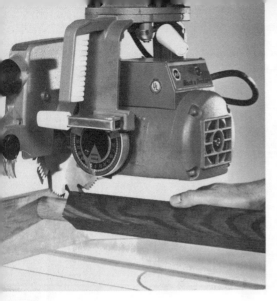

CUTTING RINGS AND PEGS. Circular stock can be made from square material as shown here. Replace the standard guide fence with a higher auxiliary one and place the motor in the in-rip position. A pivot pin—a small nail—may be driven through the fence at the desired location and the stock to be rounded pushed onto it exactly at center. The dado head can be lowered into the material by the elevating control and the material turned on the pivot point into the rotation of the dado.

CUTTING MOLDING. Many attractive moldings can be cut with the dado head. For instance, the castellated or dentil molding illustrated here is easy to make with a dado. After laying out the design and cutting it, the material can be ripped to the desired width.

LATTICE WORK. Grille or lattice work cutting is a simple matter of making a series of parallel angular cuts half way through the board. It's a good idea to lay out the design on scrap lumber and see how it looks before cutting on good boards. Actually, the designs that can be cut with the dado head are limited only by your ingenuity. First make a series of dado cuts on one side of the board. Then turn the board over and make another matching series of dado cuts. This gives the lattice effect.

CHAPTER 4

SHAPING AND JOINTING

The shaper attachments are used for straight and irregular shaping, matched shaping, tongue-and-groove cutting, planing, sizing, jointing, chamfer cutting, and making drop-leaf hinged joints. It is easy to do all these operations, and to do them quickly and accurately. The radial-arm machine's tilting-arbor shaper offers many advantages over the conventional shaper. Unlike the radial-arm shaper, standard makes have no provision for tilting the arbor or cutter head. This ability, coupled with the normal raising and lowering of the cutting head and forward and back movement of the motor carriage, adds about 50 percent more shapes to each cutter. Also, the radial-arm shaper can work in the center of wide stock—something that is impossible with the limited spindle capacity of the ordinary shaper.

Shaping may be divided into four main classifications, according to the methods used in holding or guiding the material against the cutters:

■ Holding the stock against the guide fence. This method is used for cutting stock with straight edges or faces. For underside work a sheet of plywood on the table elevates the piece enough to permit the cut. Nail a strip to the edge of the plywood so part of it replaces the guide fence and part extends above the table and is used as the fence.

■ Holding and guiding stock against the shaper ring. This is used principally for cutting stock with curved edges or faces and irregular shapes.

■ Cutting stock by following patterns. This method is used in production work when many identical pieces have to be made.

■ Holding stock on special jigs. This method is generally used for stock that cannot readily be held except on special jigs.

Before starting to work on the shaper, memorize the safety rules listed below:

■ Remove your necktie and roll up your sleeves.

■ Use the shaper fence and the safety tool guard whenever possible.

■ Remove all tools and materials from the table top before turning on the power.

■ Check the entire set up and see that the arbor rotates freely before turning on the power.

■ Feed the work into the rotation of the knives.

■ Never "back up" any work because it may be thrown out of your hands. It is better to start the operation all over again.

■ Don't attempt to shape small pieces that cannot be held safely.

■ Don't take your eyes off the work for a moment.

■ Keep the work between the cutter and your hands in such a position that a slip will not throw the hands against the cutter.

■ Cross-grained woods, or woods shaped against the grain, sometimes split or sliver on the short grain. When this occurs, the work slips rapidly past the cutters. The hands must be kept in a position to clear the cutters when this occurs.

■ Unlike a saw blade, which removes a small amount of material, a molding cutter takes a big bite. Never force the work through the cutter or try to cut too deeply.

■ Keep the cutters sharp at all times. A grinder-hone attachment is ideal for this purpose.

SHAPER-CUTTER SHAPES. There are many cutting-knife shapes available. Standard cutters, however, are each designed to do a specific job and usually require use of the full contour of the blade. These can cut shaped edges for glue joints, door lips, tongue-and-groove joints, drop-leaf tables, and quarter-round molding. The more common types of cutter profiles are shown on the next page and you can start your collection of knives with a few basic types, adding new ones as you need them. There are combination blades that permit different cuts, depending on which part of the contour is used. With these, you can shape table edges, make your own moldings, and do many other decorative jobs. It is also a good idea to cut the full profile shape of each knife as soon as you buy it and to keep it for reference. Then you can easily tell, without practice cuts, what knife, or what part of the knife, you need.

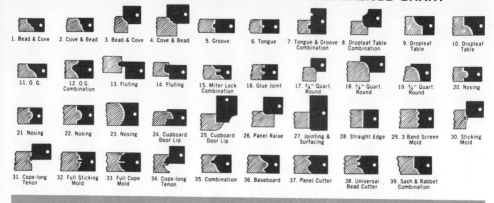

1. Bead & Cove 2. Cove & Bead 3. Bead & Cove 4. Cove & Bead 5. Groove 6. Tongue 7. Tongue & Groove Combination 8. Dropleaf Table Combination 9. Dropleaf Table 10. Dropleaf Table

11. O. G. 12. O.G. Combination 13. Fluting 14. Fluting 15. Miter Lock Combination 16. Glue Joint 17. ¾" Quart. Round 18. ⅝" Quart. Round 19. ¾" Quart. Round 20. Nosing

21. Nosing 22. Nosing 23. Nosing 24. Cupboard Door Lip 25. Cupboard Door Lip 26. Panel Raise 27. Jointing & Surfacing 28. Straight Edge 29. 3 Band Screen Mold 30. Sticking Mold

31. Cope-long Tenon 32. Full Sticking Mold 33. Full Cope Mold 34. Cope-long Tenon 35. Combination 36. Baseboard 37. Panel Cutter 38. Universal Bead Cutter 39. Sash & Rabbet Combination

MOUNTING THE MOLDING HEAD. There are two types of molding heads available for shaping. One is the detachable knife type mounted in a safety head (two styles are illustrated—top right and bottom left), and the other is the solid type (top left). The latter is milled from a solid bar of hardened and properly tempered tool steel, ground to the required shape. The detachable knives are held in the head by socket-head screws. The spindle moves clockwise so all cutters must point in the same direction. To mount the two-wing solid cutter, both arbor collars are installed before the two-winged cutter and arbor nut. For the two knife safety head, install one arbor collar, cutter head, and arbor nut. To mount the three knife head, place inside collar on arbor. Place reducer bushing (¾-inch to ⅝-inch x 9/16-inch long) on arbor. Install assembled head on arbor. Place outside collar on arbor and lock with arbor nut. The special tool guard (see page 46) should be used when shaping.

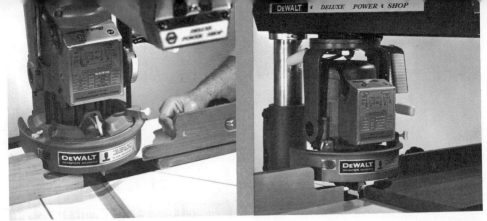

INSTALLING THE SHAPER-JOINTER
FENCE. A shaper-jointer fence is available for the radial-arm machine and should be used for straight shaping. This fence replaces the standard guide fence and fits directly into the standard guide slot. Mount the wooden (outfeed) part of the shaper fence on the left side of the table, with the metal (infeed) portion on the right. The infeed side of the fence is adjustable for any capacity up to a full ½ inch, while the outfeed side remains in a fixed position. This, of course, is of prime importance in the jointing operation when a portion of the surface of the lumber is being removed. Because the infeed side of the fence can be recessed for the exact amount of stock being removed by the jointer, there is always full support of the lumber both before and after contact with the cutting knives. The result is a smooth, clean surface, free from "ripples" and "dimples." Since the fence is designed for insertion in the guide slot of the radial-arm machine, either the infeed or outfeed side can be independently moved closer to the center of the table or toward the ends. This flexibility allows the user to place the center ends of the fence up to within ⅛ inch of the cutting diameter of the shaping or jointing knives, no matter what that diameter may be. Be sure to align both halves of the fence with a straightedge. If the entire edge must be shaped, the front half or infeed side of the fence will have to be set back an amount equal to the depth of the cut so that the molded edge will ride on the other half after it is completed.

STRAIGHT SHAPING. While most straight shaping is done with the shaper-jointer fence, you can replace the standard fence with two pieces of wood separated at the center to clear the cutters. In making any molded edge, the pattern is usually made on the edge of the work. The proper cutter is then mounted on the motor shaft, after which the arbor is raised or lowered to the proper height. This is done by adjusting the elevating handle. The work should always be fed from the right side into and against the cutters. Never force the work past the cutters or try to cut too deeply. Be sure to keep the piece on the table, because the slightest lifting will cause the cutter to gouge into the work. On very deep cuts, make several passes, adjusting the height of the knife after each one, to attain the full depth of cut required. The final pass should be a fine cut to give smoothness. If the machine stalls, vibrates, makes it hard to hold the work steady, or throws out chunks of wood instead of fine shavings, you are trying to cut too heavily. Make trial cuts in scrap wood before cutting actual parts. This is especially important when you are using matching pairs of cutters, such as for panel inserts, window sash, or tongue-and-groove joints. The mating cutters must line up perfectly or the joints will be spoiled. If the fit is tricky and you are in doubt, it is best to make the cuts on slightly thicker stock, join them, and then trim off the excess wood. Feed with the grain when possible, to minimize splintering.

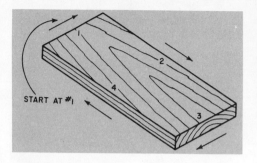

FOUR SIDE SHAPING. When cutting all edges of a piece, the first cut should be made across the end grain. Follow the procedure shown in the diagram —starting at point 1. Each edge should be taken in turn so that the final cut is with the grain. When cutting across the grain, use a pusher board or backing board of the same thickness to push the board past the cutters. This eliminates splintering of the edge and provides greater safety. Never stand directly in back of the cutter. Hold the work firmly against the fence and table with the left hand and feed the work slowly into the revolving cutter, with your right hand applying the forward pressure.

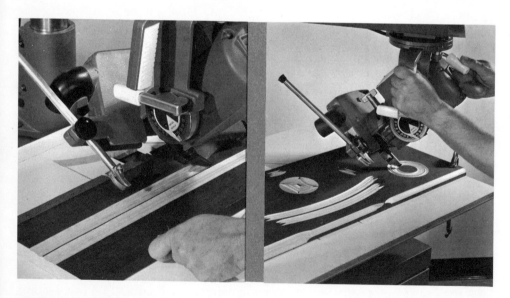

SURFACE SHAPING. As shown here, it is possible to cut moldings on the surface with the radial-arm machine. This method is ideal for applying decorative patterns on wood paneling. Place the motor in the bevel inrip position, locate it on the arm at the spot where the cut is to appear, lock the rip clamp, and lower the column to the desired depth of cut. Feed the material into and against the cutter from the right side of the table. The safety guard should be used over the shaper head. Reeding and fluting combinations can be made in this manner (left). You can also make a wide variety of ornamental molding or wood surface designs giving the appearance of hand carved work (above) by employing the top-side cutting technique. For this operation, the material is clamped to the table top and the cutter moved to make the cuts.

56

ND SHAPING. Both underside and pside shaping can be done in the andard crosscut manner. To make a old cut across the end grain and nderside of a piece of work with the adial machine, block up the work, amp a stopblock to the fence or ble, and advance the motor, feeding orward. In topside shaping, the depth f the molding is limited in this posion by the projection of the blades nd the motor clearance above the orkpiece. For angle cuts in either pe, swing the radial arm to the ngle of the mitered end of the workiece.

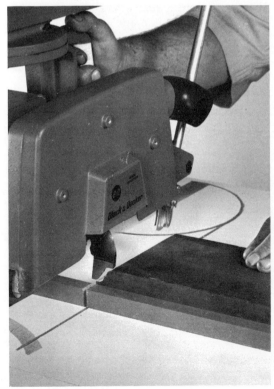

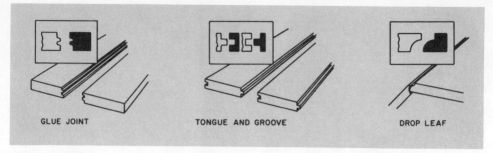

GLUE JOINT   TONGUE AND GROOVE   DROP LEAF

JOINTS. Glue, tongue-and-groove, rule or drop-leaf joints, etc. can be made with cutterhead knives as shown above. For the *glue* joint, the work must be exactly centered on the cutter. Properly centered, any two pieces will fit together when one piece is reversed end to end. When the work has a definite face side, the reversal is done after cutting, molding one piece with the face side next to the table, and the joining piece with the face side away from the table. The *tongue-and-grove* joint is run with two cutters, one making the groove and the other the tongue. Both cutters are the same length so that, when the depth setting is made for one, the same setting is used for the other. All work is done in the same position; that is, with the face side to the table. Tongue-and-groove cutters can also be used for drawer and corner joints. A *rule or drop-leaf* joint is used on tables with folding leaves. It is rather hard to make by hand, but on a shaper it can be done easily and quickly. A table usually has two leaves, each hinged to the center sec-

tion which is fastened to the legs. When laying out the rule joint, first set a marking gauge to half the thickness of the knuckle of the hinge and gauge the ends of the boards. The centers of both the concave and convex cuts lie in the gauge lines. The radius is the distance from the gauge lines to the upper surface, less $\frac{3}{4}$ inch for the square edge. Select a cutter that will fit the convex curve and cut both edges of the fixed top. The cutter for the concave cuts in the leaves should be the reverse of the first cutter, but with a radius $\frac{1}{32}$ inch larger so there will be clearance for the two moving wood parts. (Combination cutters are also available.) Turn the top and leaves upside down and place them flat on a bench. The kinds of hinges used are called "backflaps" and have one leaf longer than the other (page 123). As screw holes are countersunk on the reverse side of the hinge, the knuckles must be set into the wood. If it is difficult to obtain the correct type of hinges, ordinary hasp hinges may be used.

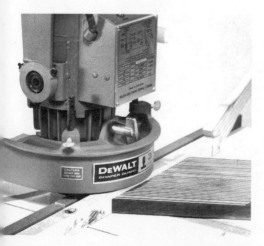

JIG FOR CUTTING NARROW STOCK. When cutting narrow stock, a feather board jig will help to support the material. To make the feather board (left), cut a miter approximately 30° across the end of a board 8 x 24 inches. Then make a series of saw kerfs about 6 inches long, with the grain of the wood. Space the kerf cuts about $\frac{3}{8}$ inch apart. Clamp jig on table as illustrated. Always use pusher to feed material.

SHAPER RING. To allow the shaping head to follow irregular curves, the standard guide fence must be removed from the table top. Then, to maintain the stock in proper relation to the cutting knives, a circular guide ring the same diameter as the cutting circle of the head must be provided. You can make a variety of these rings for your own use. As shown at the top, it is easy to construct a shaping ring. To determine the diameter, measure the shortest distance between the cutting surfaces of the opposing shaper knives. This will ensure that the stock will enter the knives to an exact and uniform dimension. The inner circle of wood is removed from the ring to allow the motor shaft to project below the surface. The shaper ring is then nailed to a small piece of 1-inch scrap lumber which replaces the standard guide when the machine is to be used for this operation (left). This shaper ring works very satisfactorily with the two-knife type shaper head.

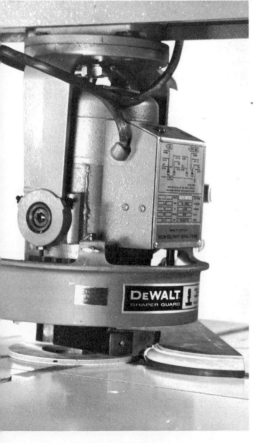

SETTING-UP FOR IRREGULAR SHAPING.
This is the shaping of the irregular edges of oval-shaped tables, curved legs, chair and table stretchers, and decorative moldings on curved edges. To set up the machine for irregular shaping, tilt the motor to the vertical position (with the cutting tool horizontal). In order to allow the shaping head to follow irregular curves, move the guide fence to the right side of the center of the table. Then, to maintain the stock in proper relation to the cutting knives, use a shaper guide ring the same diameter as the cutting circle of the head. The shaper ring, used in place of the guide fence, allows the stock to be turned freely beneath the cutting knives. In setting up the shaper, the positioning of the motor is determined by (1) the amount and position of the cutting surface to be utilized on each shaper and (2) the decision of the operator to shape the work with an undercut or an overcut. When you have decided on the direction of rotation, place the cutter and spacer collar in position and adjust the column for height. The depth of the cut is limited by the diameter of the spacer collar. The collar must be free of the resinous and charred substance that tends to accumulate on its surface; if it is not clean, it will make an uneven molding. Remember that the work will rest against the edge of the guide fence before it enters the cut.

IRREGULAR SHAPING. Some judgment is necessary in selecting the place to start a cut. It isn't always possible or advisable to begin at the end of the stock. Frequently it is necessary to select a point along the side in order to favor cross grain or to prevent the molding from splitting out the end grain. When the place of entry has been determined, hold the stock firmly on the table, clear of the cutter, with the edge resting against the fence. The corner of the fence is used as the fulcrum or starting point. Advance the work along so that the edge, at the point of entry, is tangent to the cutting circle of the blade. As soon as the stock rests firmly against the collar, swing it clear of the fence and run with no other bearing than the collar. Don't try to rest the stock against the collar and the fence after the cut has been started because it is difficult to hold in this position. Once away from the collar, the work tends to be thrown back as the cutters bite in. When you reach the point for turning the corner, swing the stock until the point rides on the left front of the collar with the unshaped edge tangent to the collar. During this shift, keep the stock moving steadily forward in firm contact with the collar. This is the secret of successful freehand shaping. When you reach the bottom of the curve, shift the pressure to the right-hand side of the collar and pull the stock straight out. Shape the remaining corners and curves in a similar manner until you reach the starting point. When cutting against the grain, feed the work very slowly. The interior edges of curved frames are shaped in the same way. The edge of the guide fence, located where it is convenient for swinging the inner side of the work against the cutter, is used.

PATTERN SHAPING. Patterns are used as guides when several pieces of the same shape have to be made or when the whole edge of a table top has to be shaped or rounded. The pattern must be the exact shape of the article wanted. Make the pattern of plywood, hardboard, or hardwood. Cut it to conform to the outline of the work, sand all edges smooth, and rub a little paraffin wax into them. Place the work face down on the table top. Place the pattern on the work and drive several small wire nails or brads through it and about $1/16$ inch into the work to prevent the pattern from slipping. Adjust the collar and cutter for the desired depth of cut. The shaper collar rests against the finished edge of the pattern, and the machine can cut into the work only as far as the pattern will permit. The pattern is guided against the collar, and the work may be placed on its underside. The front edge of the guide fence is used as a starting point as described previously for irregular shaping.

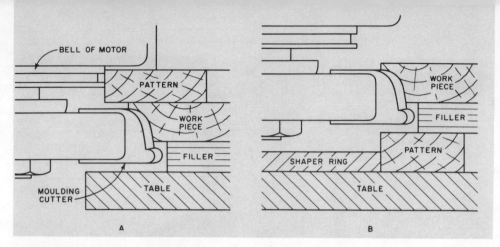

UNDERCUT PATTERN SHAPING.

For undercutting pattern molding work, a filler should be used between the pattern itself and the work in order to lift the piece for shaping the underside or the entire edge. The pattern and the workpiece must line up. The filler is bradded to both the workpiece and the pattern. The bell of the motor also can be used as a collar. Since the diameter at the neck of the motor is less than that of the molding-head assembly, the pattern must be made correspondingly oversized. This stationary guide only scores a little and won't burn the edge. A plywood filler, clamped to the table top, lifts the work above the table enough to permit shaping underneath, and cutter guarding is almost perfect.

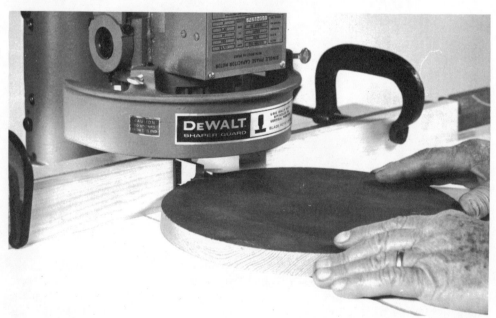

JIG SHAPING.

Some shaping jobs can be done with a simple jig. To shape the edge of round or circular stock, make a V-jig by cutting 45° bevels on two pieces of 2- or 3-inch wide board stock. Then clamp these pieces of wood to the guide fence as shown here. The space between the beveled portions can be adjusted back and forth until the proper V is obtained. The material to be cut can then be rotated as it is held against the V-block. The circle jig shown on page 81 can be used in circular shaping. Locate the jig on the table, clamp it to the top, and fasten the stock on the pivot point. Rotate the disk into the rotation of the cutter. With this jig a roughly sawed disk is easily molded to the desired dimensions of a circle.

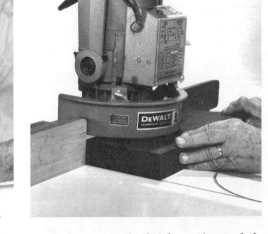

MOUNTING JOINTING CUTTERS. To install the jointer, remove everything from the arbor shaft. Then slide on the jointer and tighten the special adapter nut which comes with the jointer blade. Use the wrenches provided. Now place the motor in the vertical position and set it on the radial arm so the lead portions of the jointer blades line up with the rear or outfeed fence. Lower the motor to the desired depth by means of the elevating handle. The 2-inch straightedge jointing or surfacing shaper knives can also be used in the same way as the four-wing jointer.

EDGE JOINTING. When jointing, it is most important to position the cutters correctly in relation to the shaper-jointer fence. Replace the regular guide fence with the shaper-jointer fence. Be careful to adjust the in-feed side of the fence and the cutting edge of the jointer blades so that they are in a straight line with the out-feed side of the fence. Then adjust the in-feed fence for the depth of cut by moving it back, using the scale. When properly adjusted, attach the tool guard. Feed the material from right to left, applying pressure firmly against the in-feed fence and table.

When the material has passed about half way through the cutters, apply pressure on the out-feed fence. Applying pressure at the proper place is important because it prevents the material from sliding into the opening in the fence. As you can see, this opening is around the cutting tool. Generally, it is best to joint no more than $1/16$ inch at a time. It is safer to make two passes rather than attempt a full $1/8$ inch cut in one pass. Feed material slowly. Be sure the tool guard is adjusted so that the material will just slide under it.

SIZING. To perform this operation, you need the simple jig shown at the left. The exact width of the finished stock is determined by measuring the distance between the front guide and the cutters. Lock the carriage at the desired position on the arm. Feed the stock into the cutters from the right side of the table. Apply pressure against guide fence on the front of jig. This sizing operation give you the desired width and a jointed edge all in one operation.

MOUNTING ROTARY SURFACER. This attachment will quickly and efficiently cut warped boards down to uniform thickness and convert them into usable stock ready for sanding or finishing. To install the rotary surfacer, remove all items from the motor shaft. Screw on the rotary surfacer directly to the motor shaft. Tilt the motor to the vertical position (the surfacer will be in a horizontal position), adjust the motor on the arm where the surfacing is to be done, lock the rip clamp, and lower the column until the surfacer knives project slightly below the top surface of the material.

ROTARY SURFACING METHOD NO. 1. To use the rotary surfacer for this operation, place the stock flat on the table against the fence and feed the work into the rotary surfacer from right to left, following the grain. For wide pieces, make successive cuts at the same depth setting; move the motor on the arm. Keep the work flat on the table to prevent gouging. When the top side is surfaced flat, turn the piece over and surface it parallel with the first side. Plane bevel edges by setting the motor at the desired angle.

ROTARY SURFACING METHOD NO. 2. Rotary surfacing can also be done with the jointing-surfacing knives in the two-knife head. These knives are sharpened on two edges. The set-up for this method is the same as outlined in Method No. 1. It is safer and more efficient to take a light cut, about $1/16$ inch on each pass. Feed the material slowly from right to left, applying a light, steady pressure.

CHAMFER CUTTING AND PANEL RAISING. It is possible to cut chamfers (left) and do panel raising (bottom left) with any shaper head and straight-edge knives. These operations are accomplished by placing the motor in either the in- or out-rip position (the former preferred) and setting it in a bevel position. Any degree of angle can be placed on the edge of the stock simply by changing the bevel angle of the motor. Place the material against the fence, place the motor at the proper location on the radial arm, and lower the column to the proper depth of cut. Feed the material slowly past the knives in the same manner as when ripping. When panel raising, as in other cuts where the work is molded on all sides, the end cuts should be run first so that the final cuts with the grain will clean up the work. Actually any molding pattern desired can be cut on an angle or bevel.

RABBETING. This operation can be done with any of the molding cutterheads and straightedge knives, as shown here. This method is easier than the two-saw cut method and is especially good for shallow cuts. For deep rabbet cuts, make several shallow cuts lowering the cutter after each.

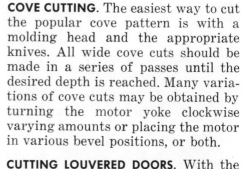

COVE CUTTING. The easiest way to cut the popular cove pattern is with a molding head and the appropriate knives. All wide cove cuts should be made in a series of passes until the desired depth is reached. Many variations of cove cuts may be obtained by turning the motor yoke clockwise varying amounts or placing the motor in various bevel positions, or both.

CUTTING LOUVERED DOORS. With the two-knife shaper head and the jointing-surfacing knives, a louvered effect can be formed in solid material, as shown at the left. Install the shaper head and knives on the arbor shaft. Tilt the motor to a 90° bevel position as you would in horizontal shaping. Now tilt the motor beyond 90° (it might be 5° to 10° beyond) depending on the angle of the louvers desired. Place material on the table and adjust the machine for the desired depth of cut, generally ¼ inch. Make successive cuts, as in surfacing. Guide the motor along the arm the desired distance for the spacing of the louvers. It is best to make the first cut on the forward portion of the material (toward the front of the machine table) and work toward the rear with each successive cut. When finished, trim the panel to size and frame. You now have a solid louvered door.

CHAPTER 5

BORING AND ROUTING

The radial-arm machine allows unlimited boring capacity. Equipped with the boring-bit attachments, it overcomes many limitations of the conventional drill press. For example, there is no restriction on the length or width of material you can bore because of the size of the throat opening or the length of the press downstroke. The boring action of the radial-arm machine is horizontal rather than vertical. Thus, material several feet in length can be end bored with precision and accuracy. The depth of the hole to be bored is limited only by the length of the bit itself, not by the stroke of the press. The machine's accuracy, permits the use of dowel joints—one of the best for countless shop jobs.

For boring, a chuck is necessary to hold the bit. Conventional right-hand wood bits of the proper shank size may be used with your radial–arm machine.

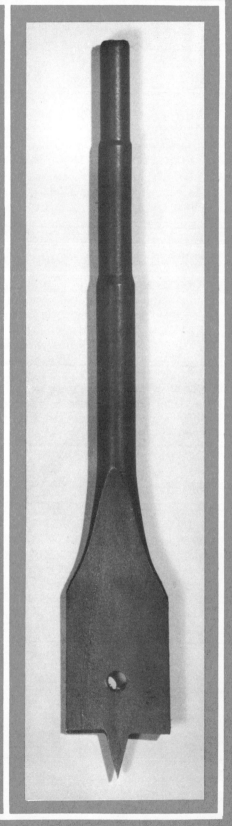

Accurate layout is a basic requirement of boring. The easiest method of marking the location for a hole is to draw two lines which intersect at the desired spot. A combination square is ideal for such work, since it can be used to draw lines parallel with the edge of the work and as an edgemarking gauge. Dividers are handy when it is necessary to transfer a measurement from one piece of wood to another or to mark off a number of equal spaces. If a pencil is used for marking, select a hard one (3H or harder) and keep it sharp so the lines will be well defined.

Safety practices for the boring operation of the radial-arm machine are the same as for all other accessories. In addition, observe the following:

■ Keep fingers away from the revolving tool.

■ Never remove chips with your fingers.

■ The boring bit must be secure in the chuck.

■ Keep cutting bits sharp.

■ Use a "C" clamp to limit the depth of boring.

WOOD-BORING JIG. For various boring operations use a simple jig (drawing below) to raise the material above the table top and to provide a higher guide fence. Place a wedge between the jig and column for support when boring. A flat board about 6 inches in height may also be employed as a boring jig and should be inserted in place of the standard guide fence. This jig is good for most face boring operations.

MOUNTING THE BORING BIT. To assemble the boring bit and chuck, first remove the safety guard, the arbor nut, the cutting tool, and the arbor collars from the motor arbor. Put the boring bit in the chuck and tighten it in place with the key provided. Insert the Allen wrench in the front end of the arbor, holding it secure while turning the right-hand threaded chuck on the back of the motor shaft with the right hand. For all face boring operations, be sure to mount the safety guard on the motor to cover the front end arbor. This will assure maximum protection at all times.

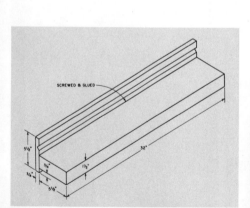

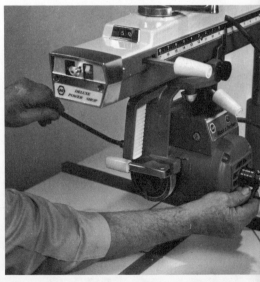

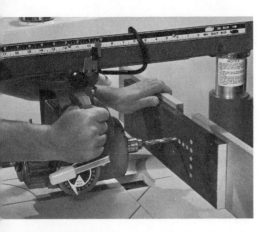

FACE BORING. Locate the center of the hole and mark it with a center punch or scratch. Bring the motor forward to the front of the arm and swing it to the out-rip position (the bit will face toward the column of the ma-chine). Set your material on edge on the boring jig and against the guide fence. Raise or lower the arm so the bit touches the stock at the desired spot. Turn on the machine and slowly push the yoke assembly backward on the arm until the bit has entered the stock to the desired depth. Hold the stock firmly and apply even pressure to the yoke. If the stock is hardwood, or the hole is deep, back out the bit once or twice to remove the chips before finishing the hole. If you plan to bore all the way through the board, place a piece of scrap wood behind the hole and against the high guide fence. This will prevent splintering as the bit goes through the wood. A "C" clamp can be fastened to the radial arm to serve as a stop to limit the depth of the hole.

EDGE BORING. Place the material flat on the jig and against the fence. With the motor in the out-rip position, raise or lower the arm until the desired location is obtained. Push the yoke assembly back on the arm until the hole has been bored to the correct depth. Use slow, even pressure. Back out the bit once or twice to remove the chips. For boring more than one hole of the same depth, you can place a stop (rip) clamp on the arm to limit the travel of the head.

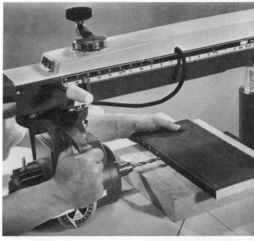

PARALLEL BORING. This is merely making a series of holes in the manner described for face boring. Because the stock remains positioned at exactly the same level on the boring jig and the bit enters at exactly the same height (riding on machined tracks inside the arm), there can never be any question as to whether the holes will be parallel to one another. As shown, parallel boring can be done in the vertical direction, too. Keep the depth constant by lowering and raising the arm with the elevating handle the same number of turns.

ANGULAR OR RADIUS BORING. The stock is positioned on the jig exactly as for face boring. The radial arm, however, is moved either to the right or left so the bit will enter the stock at an angle when pushed back on the arm. The calibrated miter scale on the arm allows you to determine the angle at which the bit will enter. Angular boring can also be accomplished by placing the stock in a V-groove in the auxiliary table and boring in the same manner as when face boring. Angular boring is used for such things as drilling dowel holes on tilted furniture legs.

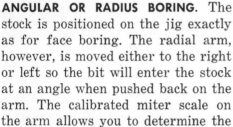

BORING IN ROUND STOCK. Round work can be pushed tight against the fence and jig table, or a V–block and held as shown above. The hole is then drilled as described in face boring. To bore holes around a curve, either on a circle or some other shape, pivot the work on the center of the circle, using a bolt through the piece or a nail filed to a sharp point and driven into an auxiliary table. The V–block can also be used when boring the corner of a square leg for a lag screw.

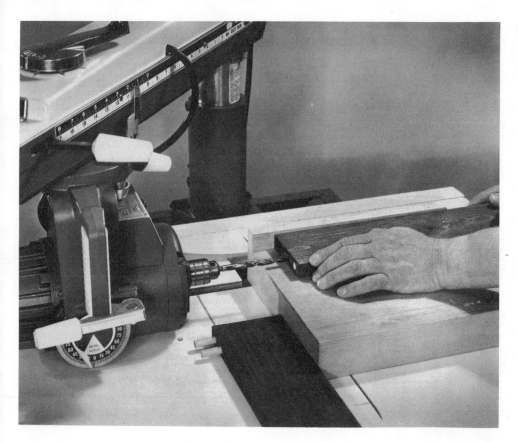

END BORING. Place the material flat on the auxiliary table and against the fence. The radial arm can be placed in the 15° left miter position to give you more room on the right side of the table. The motor and boring bit should be parallel to the guide fence and located on the arm so the bit touches the stock at the desired spot. Lock the motor in place with the rip clamp. Then push the stock into the bit until the hole is the desired depth. On deep holes, back off from the bit once or twice to remove the chips. A stop block can be clamped to the guide fence on the auxiliary table to limit depth of the hole.

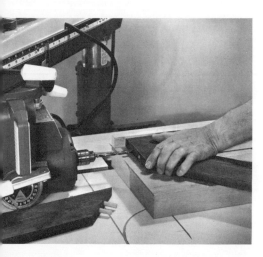

MITER BORING. Miter joints are often strengthened with dowels. Using the same jig and with the motor placed exactly as for end boring, just push the stock into the bit at any desired angle. Use a "pusher" board with a mitered end to direct the stock into the bit at the proper angle. Note that since the bit remains stationary, it is possible to bore holes in the same position on the ends of more than one piece of stock. When moving for a second hole, the rip scale on the right of the arm makes accurate placing of the bit an easy job.

ATTACHING THE ROUTER BIT. The mounting of the router bit on the recessed side of the motor (right side) is relatively simple. It involves three basic attachments—the chuck, chuck key, and desired router bit.

Merely screw the chuck into the recessed end of the motor shaft. Screw it clockwise to tighten. It is a good idea to insert the arbor hex wrench on the left end of the motor, supporting it against the guide fence. This keeps the shaft from turning while tightening the chuck. Then use the chuck key to apply sufficient leverage to tighten the chuck in place. This simply means that after you tighten the chuck with your fingers, one good downward turn using the chuck key for leverage should be sufficient.

Open the chuck jaws to the desired dimension to accept the router bit shank, insert the bit and tighten with the chuck key so that the jaws clamp securely around the shank in the same manner as when positioning a drill bit in a conventional portable electric drill.

Make sure you remove the hex wrench from the left end of the motor shaft. Then raise the radial arm, loosen the bevel clamp, and place the motor in vertical position.

The following pages will show you the efficiency of routing as a specialized but important accessory on the radial-arm machine.

More significant routing applications with a portable router can be seen in the special chapter on portable power tools.

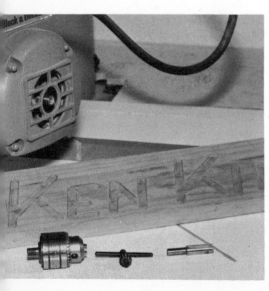

ROUTING. The radial-arm boring machine can be quickly converted into a router by changing bits. There are two general classifications of routing —straight and irregular. Straight work is done against a fence; irregular work can be cut freehand or with a pattern. In either case, the work feed must be against the rotation of the cutter. This means the material being cut is fed from left to right. The depth of all routing should be 1/8 inch or less per pass; if a deeper cut is desired, make it with multiple cuts.

STRAIGHT ROUTING. This is done with a guide fence. With the motor in the 90° bevel position (the shaft in a vertical location), set it for the desired width of the cut and lock the rip-clamp. Lower the arm by means of the elevating handle to the depth of the cut. Turn the machine on and, keeping the work pressed firmly against the fence, move it slowly past the cutting tool.

RABBET CUTTING. In rabbet cutting, the standard guide fence should be replaced with two pieces of wood separated at the center to allow room for the router to rotate. The shaper-jointer fence will serve the same purpose. Rabbeting is done the same way as straight routing. Remember, never attempt to make more than a 1/8-inch cut at a time. If a greater depth is desired, lower the arm one turn of the handle for each pass. For rabbets wider than the bit, move the motor forward on the arm so the cuts just overlap each other. Clamp the motor in position and push the stock past the router bit. Continue this movement away from the fence until the required width is obtained.

ROUTING CURVED OR ROUND WORK. Two methods of routing grooves in curved or round work are shown here. In each case a guide block is clamped to the table and the motor is positioned to make the cut where it is needed. If the work is saber-sawed carefully, the waste stock can be utilized as the guide for the work. Be sure to hold the work firmly as you move it around the guide in a clockwise direction.

CROSS ROUTING. Dadoes can also be cut with the router bit. In this operation the work remains stationary and the bit is moved through it. With the stock against the fence and the router bit behind it, pull the yoke slowly forward in the same way as for crosscutting. Several passes may be necessary to get the desired width and depth.

ORNAMENTAL ROUTING. Any number of ornamental molding designs can be made with a router. It's a simple matter to cross–rout with the work butted against the guide fence. To assure even spacing of the cuts, mark the proper distance on the fence as described for saw kerfing (page 31). Use a stop clamp on the arm to limit the travel of the router when making repeat cuts.

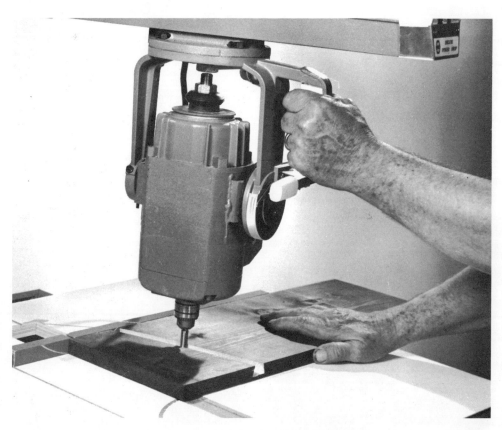

ANGULAR ROUTING. With the radial arm set in the desired miter angle position and the stock placed against the fence, pull the router across the board. This angle routing operation is often used in the making of louvered screens and panels.

FREEHAND ROUTING. Signs and decorations are sometimes made freehand with the router. Carefully lay out the areas to be removed. Place the motor in the 90° bevel position and lower the arm so the depth of the bit will make the proper cut. Locate the motor on the arm at a convenient location so the work can be swung around the bit. Lock the motor in position with the rip clamp, turn on the machine, and move the work past the router, following the outline. Place a piece of hardboard under the stock for easy movement.

EDGE ROUTING. Edge grooving is accomplished by placing the material on the boring jig and setting the motor in the position for edge boring. The difference between edge boring and routing is that in the latter the material is moved past the bit instead of remaining stationary. This operation is generally used to make a *round-end mortise* for a round-end tenon. Use the fence as a guide with a stop clamp to control the length of the slot. Deep cuts should be made in several passes, moving the bit closer to the column after each pass until the full depth of the cut has been obtained.

CHAPTER 6

SABER SAWING

The saber saw adds more to the versatility of the radial-arm machine than any other tool. Scroll-cutting with a saber saw gives you all the fun of intricate fretwork, with very little effort. You just steer the piece; the machine does the work more accurately and ten times as fast as your arm could. Usable stock on a saber saw ranges from veneers $1/_{28}$–inch–thick to 2-inch–thick rough planks. Truly versatile, the saber saw turns out an unlimited variety of cutouts— garden ornaments, pierced what-nots, plaques, clock cases, silhouettes, signs made of cut-out block letters—and works on light metal and plastics.

To operate the saber saw with maximum efficiency, you should become familiar with the various blades available. For most purposes, four blades will do the job. The table below lists various materials and suggests the size saber-saw blade for cutting them.

Material	Thickness, inches	Blade size, teeth per inch
Softwood	Up to $1/_2$	15 to 20
Softwood	Over $1/_2$	7 to 10
Hardwood	Up to $1/_2$	15 to 20
Hardwood	Over $1/_2$	10 to 15
Nonferrous metal	Up to $1/_8$	20
Nonferrous metal	Over $1/_8$	15 or 20
Plastic, ivory, bone, etc.		10, 15, or 20

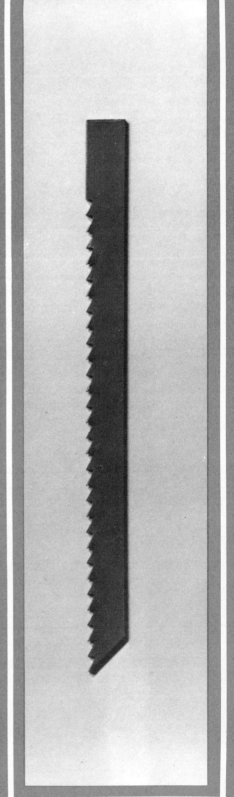

Always use the blade with the coarsest teeth which will cut the material cleanly and which will cut the sharpest curve in the pattern you are working on. As you progress with your saber sawing, your experience with various materials and blades will help you in choosing the right one for the particular operation on hand.

Since the prime purpose of the saber saw is to cut curves and patterns, it is usually desirable to lay out your work before cutting. Except for simple designs which can be sketched directly on the material, it is necessary to make a full size pattern of work and transfer it to the stock being cut. Patterns are usually drawn on paper and then transferred to the stock. If the template is to be used only once, it can be glued or cemented to the stock. Use rubber cement, mucilage, or shellac.

With rubber cement, apply a thin coat to the back of the pattern and allow it to dry a minute or two. Place the edge of the paper on the stock; then, as you lay the pattern down, smooth it out with your hands. Don't attempt to lay the entire pattern on the stock in one movement.

If mucilage is used, spread the liquid on the wood only. Apply one coat, allow a short time for it to dry, then apply a second coat before placing the pattern on the stock. Lay the pattern on as described for rubber cement.

If shellac is used, only the stock should be coated. When the shellac becomes tacky, which takes only a few minutes, roll the pattern on the stock in the same manner as you would with rubber cement.

When a pattern is to be used several times, the outline can be transferred to the stock with carbon paper. Place a sheet of carbon paper on the stock with the prepared side down and lay the pattern over it. Hold the pattern in position with several thumbtacks placed outside the area to be used. With pencil or stylus, go over the pattern outline with sufficient pressure to transfer the design through the carbon paper onto the stock. If you don't have carbon paper, the same result can be obtained by coating the back of the pattern with graphite from a soft pencil, then proceeding as outlined above.

If a design is to be used a number of times or if you want to keep it for future use, it is advisable to prepare a wood pattern. Glue the paper pattern to a piece of $\frac{1}{8}$-inch hardwood or $\frac{1}{4}$-inch plywood, then cut the outline on the saber saw. The edges should be smoothed. This type of pattern becomes a permanent piece of your shop's equipment and can be used indefinitely.

For most saber sawing, stand directly in front of the blade with both hands resting comfortably on the table. Guide the work with both hands, applying forward pressure with the thumbs. Make sure the guide fingers always rest lightly on the work.

MOUNTING THE SABER SAW. To mount the saber-saw unit, remove the safety guard, arbor nut, arbor collars and cutting tool from the motor. Slide the saber saw over the motor shaft, seating it against the motor end bell assembly. Be sure the locating pins in back of the saber saw are inserted into the holes provided, and tighten the locking studs with thumb nuts in the front rotating foot of each stud into the safety guard groove. Tighten the arbor nut. Align the saber-saw blade with the ¼-inch diameter hole in the table top by swinging the radial arm to the left and swiveling the motor yoke to the right. Then lock all controls—arm clamp, yoke clamp, and rip lock. Lower the radial arm by means of the elevating handle until the saber-saw guide barely touches the top surface of the material

to be cut. When saber sawing, the guide fence, in most operations, should be removed from its normal position and placed at the extreme rear of the table.

MOUNTING THE BLADE. To mount a saber-saw blade, loosen the Allen-head setscrew on the front of the chuck with a wrench and place the blade approximately ⅜ inch into the chuck against the insert, with the teeth pointing downward. Tighten the chuck setscrews and you are ready to start cutting.

TECHNIQUE OF CUTTING. To keep blade breakage at a minimum and to produce perfectly cut work, don't crowd the blade; that is, don't apply too much pressure as you feed the wood into the blade in an effort to speed up the cutting. Maintain steady, even pressure. Also, when cutting curves, swing the stock so the blade is at a tangent to the curve at all times. Side pressure need never be applied in order to keep the saw blade cutting on the line or parallel to it. Frequently, if a dull blade is used to cut thick hardwood, the blade will have a tendency to follow the grain and pull away from a line, no matter how you feed the stock. The remedy is to replace the blade with a sharp one. On most hardwoods and for all metals, a little

soap or wax will improve cutting and keep the blade sharp.

CUTTING EXTERNAL CURVES. Install the correct blade and lower the radial arm until the hold-down guide fingers rest lightly on top of the material (each complete turn of the elevating handle raises or lowers the arm exactly ⅛ inch). Place the work on the table with your forefinger over it on either side and the other fingers on the table. Turn on the motor and begin to cut. Start in the waste stock and come up to the layout line at a slight angle, applying as much pressure as necessary to keep the cutting going without vibration. A smooth cut is obtained only when the work is carefully guided. Don't twist the blade, as it is easily broken.

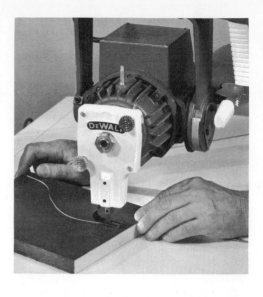

CUTTING SHARP TURNS. When cutting sharp curves, apply no forward pressure and turn the work slowly. Extremely sharp curves can be cut by first making many relief cuts to within ¹⁄₃₂ inch of the layout line. The stock will then fall away as the curve is cut. Sharp curves can also be cut by first making several auxiliary relief cuts or by making tangent cuts.

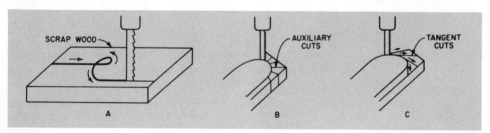

CUTTING INTERIOR SQUARE CORNERS. When it's necessary to saw to the end of a long, thin opening, cut to the corner, back out the blade a short way, and "nibble out" the corner until the work can be turned. Although a corner may be sharp, the material being cut should never be swung suddenly at a sharp angle; this will cause the blade to break. The cutting of sharp corners can be accomplished by cutting into the waste portion of the material in order to change the direction of the cut. To cut a square opening from the edge, make straight cuts to the top of the opening on one side, arc across the waste, and back out the blade. Then start at the other side and cut an arc across the waste stock to the top of the other side. Complete the cut by nibbling out the top.

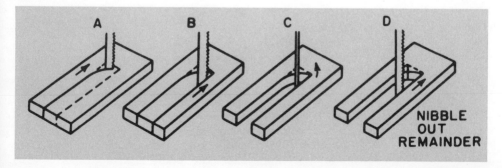

CUTTING INTERNAL OPENINGS. With a small boring bit, drill a hole in the waste stock portion of your work large enough for the blade. (Sometimes it's possible to make the hole part of the design. For example, if a rectangular opening with rounded corners is needed, bore four holes of the desired radius, one at each corner.) Elevate the radial arm by means of the elevating handle until the end of the saber-saw blade is high enough off the table to allow the stock to pass beneath it. Place the hole you have drilled in the stock directly beneath the blade; lower the arm until the fingers of the guide rest on top of your materials. Then turn on the motor and begin to cut. The

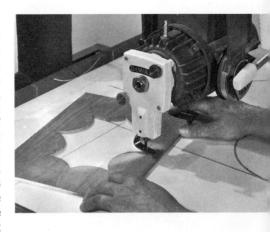

cutting technique for internal openings is the same as for external work. The machine should be stopped while scrap material is removed.

CUTTING CIRCLES AND ARCS. A circular piece can usually be cut freehand in the same manner as other curves, although it is somewhat more difficult. However, to make the task easier, it's suggested you construct the simple jig shown (left). This jig is also very valuable for sanding circular objects (see page 94). It is made of ¾-inch plywood, and the groove or dado is cut at right angles to the teeth of the blade and parallel with the guide fence. A hardwood or aluminum strip slips into the groove and is flush with the top of the auxiliary table. A sharp pin, brad, or screw is placed at the end of the sliding bar to act as the center point of the arc or circle. It is also a good idea to put a small flat-head screw next to the bar so that when it is tightened the bar will not move. The jig is placed on the guide fence and is clamped to the front of the stationary table top. Place the material on the center point and lower the blade until the guide fingers rest lightly on top of the stock. (Remember: The blade must be at right angles to the sliding bar and in line with the front.) Now adjust the pin equal to the radius of the desired circle. Switch on the machine and turn the material slowly as the circle is cut. Another easy method is shown at the right.

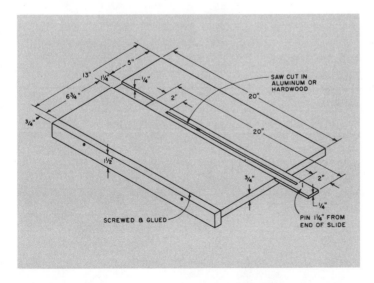

MULTIPLE CUTTING. Like the radial saw the saber type is suitable for multiple cutting. This can be done by arranging the pieces in a pile, then applying the pattern to the face of the top piece. The total thickness of such pieces, when piled one on the other, should not exceed 2 inches (the capacity of the saw). The pieces should be held together with several brads inserted in the waste wood. Thus the nails or brads will not leave holes in the finished work. Tape may also be used to hold the parts together.

BEVEL CUTTING. A bevel or chamfer can be cut by releasing the bevel clamp and moving the motor to the desired angle. Tighten the bevel clamp and you are ready to do the most intricate inside- or outside-beveled scroll work in the same manner as the external and internal cuts previously described. You can cut beveled circles on the jig described on page 81.

CUTTING GROOVES IN A DOWEL ROD. A dowel rod with slight grooves holds better for gluing because the glue can penetrate along the entire length. Swivel the motor so the saber unit is at an angle of 15° to 30° and place a V-block tight against the guide fence. Now place the dowel rod in the V and push it into the saw to the desired depth. By rotating the dowel past the blade, the saw will cut a spiral groove along the rod.

AIR HOSE FOR YOUR SABER SAW. To keep your guide line free of sawdust when cutting, you can insert a piece of flexible plastic or copper tubing in one of the air holes in the motor unit and bend the tubing as shown. A flexible tube is included in the purchase of the saber saw accessory.

LARGE WORK WITH THE SABER SAW. A major advantage of the saber saw attachment to the radial-arm machine is the size of the work which can be handled. Where the work is of such length that it will strike the column before the cut is completed, cutting from the side or using an extension table is necessary. Side cutting requires the motor to be swiveled until the blade of the saber unit is parallel with the guide fence. A 5/16-inch diameter hole should be drilled directly under the saw blade at the front of the stationary table, when the motor is completely to the front of the radial arm. This allows full capacity for large work between the saber saw blade and the column. Be sure to move the guide fence to a back position.

CHAPTER 7

LATHE IN ACTION

No other machine work is so responsive to the whim of the craftsman as wood turning. It's a fascinating art, for under the chisel, the whirling wood is molded like clay on the potter's wheel. Only your imagination limits the forms which can evolve. Table legs, lamp bases, bowls, and candlesticks shaped in countless designs are but a few of the items which can be made with a lathe.

The principal parts of a lathe are the headstock, tailstock, and tool rest. The headstock contains the driving mechanism, the step pulley for changing speeds, and the spindle. The spindle of the headstock lines up exactly with the tailstock spindle. The two main attachments are the spur center, which fits the headstock spindle and is commonly known as the "live center," and the cup center, which fits the tailstock spindle and is known as the "dead center." The work is mounted between these two centers, the spurs of the live center serving as the driving member. The faceplate is fastened to the headstock spindle in certain types of turnings in place of the spurs.

The tailstock assembly may be clamped to the bed at any position. A hand wheel can be turned to move the tailstock spindle in or out 3¼ inches.

The tool rest and holder clamp are attached to the bed and can be adjusted to various diameters of work.

There are two basic types of turning — spindle and faceplate — which are done on a lathe.

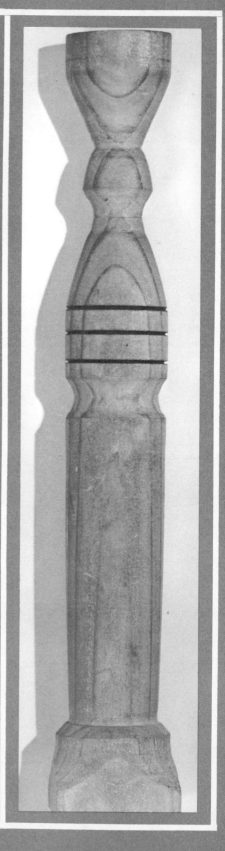

Spindle turning or turning between centers means the turning of all work held between the live and dead centers. This is the principal type of wood turning, as typified by table and chair legs, lamp stems, etc.

When the work to be turned can't be held between the live and the dead center, a faceplate is used. All cutting in faceplate work is done by scraping; any attempt to use a cutting technique on the edge grain of large work will result in a hogging, gouging cut which may tear the chisel out of your hands. The work is held to the faceplate by means of screws.

Generally speaking, the larger the work, the slower the speed. Turning large work at excessive speed is very dangerous and should never be attempted. Suitable speeds for various size turnings have been established with regard to both safety and procedure, and these should be followed. The four-step pulleys on the radial-arm lathe provide four speeds which are adequate for all your turning jobs. Position 1 (the largest diameter) gives a speed of 1,200 rpm, position 2 gives 1,540 rpm, position 3 gives 2,025 rpm, and position 4 (the smallest diameter on the lathe pulley) gives 3,040 rpm.

Speed rpm

Diameter of work, inches	Roughing cut	General cutting	Finishing
Under 3	1,540	2,025	3,040
3–6	1,200	1,540	2,025
6–8	1,200	1,540	1,540
Over 8	1,200	1,200	1,200

While the lathe is one of the safest tools to operate on your radial-arm machine, accidents can happen. Before attempting to do any work on a lathe, it is advisable to become familiar with certain precautions for your own safety.

■ Be sure the wood you are going to turn is free of knots, checks, and other defects. Don't turn stock which is badly cracked, it might come apart when run at high speed. If turning glued stock between centers, it is advisable to cut it a little longer than needed and insert a screw in both ends.

■ Fasten the work securely between the centers, or to the faceplates, and tighten the two clamps on the tailstock and tool post because work thrown from the lathe has tremendous force.

■ After tightening all the clamps, revolve the stock by hand to make sure it clears all points.

■ Remember to put soap or oil on the end running on the dead center, because the friction at this spot will usually burn the wood and its exact center may be lost. It may also become loose and fly out of the lathe.

■ Place the tool rest as close to the work as possible. Don't change its position while the lathe is running because you might injure your hand.

■ Never allow any other person to stand near the lathe when it is being operated.

■ Hold all tools firmly and use only sharp ones. Dull tools are always very dangerous to use.

■ Don't turn stock that is too far out of center, as it causes excessive vibration and may be thrown from the lathe.

MOUNTING THE LATHE. To mount the lathe, remove the guard and cutting tool. Swivel the motor to the out-rip position and swing the arm 90° to the left. Set the lathe on top of the radial-arm machine table top with the base plates of the lathe tight against the guide fence and the headstock to the left. Insert eyebolts through the hole in the L-shaped clamps and thread the eyebolts into the two holes next to the innermost holes in the base plates. Set the clamps with the long part of the L beneath the radial-arm machine table and the short part resting against the bottom of the base plate. Use the nuts on the eyebolts as adjustable shoulders and draw eyebolts tight, clamping the lathe securely in place. Then place 1¾-inch-diameter pulley shaft in place and secure it with the arbor nut. Select the desired speed

and place the drive belt in the proper pulley groove. Slip the other end of the belt over the motor pulley. Use the radial-arm rip lock, yoke clamp, and arm clamp as positioning aids.

TURNING TOOLS. The standard tools used in wood turning are shown here. The gouge (A) is used for straight turning and for cutting concave and convex surfaces. A bevel is ground on the convex side at an angle of about 30°. Skews (B) are used for finished turning, smoothing straight surfaces, cutting shoulders, trimming ends, and cutting V's and beads. They get their name from the fact that the cutting edge is askew, usually at an angle of about 60°. The tool is ground from both sides. The upper end is called the toe and the lower end the heel. Usually two sizes, 1 inch (large) and ½ inch (small), are needed. The parting tool (C) has angled sides and is pointed. The point is ground from both sides. It is used for trimming ends and for turning to various diameters. When in use, it is held on edge and forced into the work. The round nose (D) is similar to an ordinary chisel except that it is ground with a semicircular end. The bevel is on one side at an angle of about 45°.

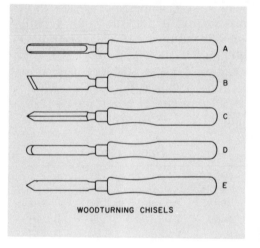

WOODTURNING CHISELS

It is used for many scraping operations such as cutting coves or large recesses. It is also used on all faceplate work. The spear or diamond point (E) is ground to a sharp point with a bevel on one side at an angle of about 45°. It is used for scraping operations such as forming sharp V's or corners.

with a prick punch or scratch awl. Remove the spur center from the headstock spindle by loosening the Allen-head screws. With a soft-faced mallet drive the spur of the headstock into the saw cut at the center point. Never drive the piece of wood against the headstock of the lathe by hammering on the far end. This will damage the bearing on the lathe and eventually will knock the headstock out of correct alignment. Replace the spur center on the headstock spindle and tighten the setscrews. Lubricate the dead center of the tailstock with oil, or if the stain is objectionable, fill the cup with soap, paraffin, or other solid lubricant so the stock will not be burned by friction. Move the tailstock of the lathe so its point of dead center is approximately ½ inch from the end of the stock. Secure the tailstock in place by tightening with wrench and adjust the tool rest ⅛ inch above center. Then, continue by turning the handwheel of the tailstock so the dead center will be set in the stock so firmly that the work cannot be turned by hand. Turn the handwheel in the opposite direction just enough so the work can now be turned by hand. Tighten the dead–center clamp at the top of the tailstock.

MOUNTING THE STOCK. To make mounting easier, make two diagonal saw cuts across the end that is to be at the headstock of the lathe. If the wood is extremely hard, saw a kerf about ⅛ inch deep across each corner and drill a small center hole, ¹/₁₆ inch in diameter and ⅛ inch deep, in either end for insertion of the centers. In soft woods, mark the center

---

SHAPING SQUARE STOCK INTO A CYLINDER. The first step in shaping a rectangular piece into a cylinder on the lathe is called roughing. Hold the gouge firmly and run the lathe at the speed recommended on page 85. Place the convex side of the gouge against the tool rest about 2 inches from the dead center. (Never start a cut at the end of the stock; the cutting tool is apt to catch and be forcibly thrown from your hand). The index finger or your wrist should be held firmly against the rest and the cutting tool against the top. Twist the turning tool slightly to the right and force it into the revolving stock until cutting begins. The beveled edge should be tangent to the cylinder. Then push the tool slowly toward the tailstock. Start the second

cut several inches to the left of the first and continue in the direction of the first cut until both meet. When rounding off material, do not take long cuts; large chips or slivers of wood are apt to fly off, causing injury to you or the material.

LAYING OUT SPINDLE WORK. When the stock has been turned to a perfect cylindrical form of the required dimensions, it is ready for turning or forming to any desired shape or combination of shapes that constitutes a finished piece. Make a full-size drawing of the desired turning. Then determine the points where the shoulder or sizing cuts are to be made and mark them on the drawing. With a pair of dividers, transfer these points from the drawing and locate them on the cylinder. Place the point of a pencil on each of the marks made by the dividers and revolve the cylinder by hand to mark the entire circumference. Adjust the calipers for a diameter $1/16$ inch larger than required, as shown in the drawing or pattern, for the point where the first shoulder or sizing cut is to be made.

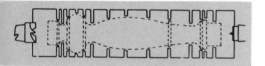

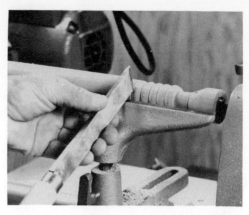

CUTTING A LINE. The simplest ornament for a spindle turning is an incised line. After the cylinder has been cut, set the tool rest about level with the lathe center, touch a lead pencil against the revolving work. Rest the skew on its edge with the toe down and the handle lowered. Lift the handle until the point digs in and the incised line is made. A shallow line can also be made when the cylinder is scraped with a diamond-point chisel laid flat on the tool rest.

CUTTING A SHOULDER. Hold the small skew on edge with the toe down and the heel up; it should be at a slight angle so one bevel is at a right angle to the cylinder. Force the skew into the wood a little at a time; then remove it and cut a half V groove until the smaller diameter is reached with a small gouge. Place the skew on its side and trim to the smaller diameter. Use the heel of the skew to cut to the corner.

CHECKING YOUR CUTS. To check if your cuts are being made to the proper diameter, use a pair of calipers. Adjust them to a diameter $1/16$-inch greater than required for the finished work. This allowance is made for the finishing cuts and final sanding. With the calipers in your left hand and the chisel in the right, make your cut. As the work progresses, use the calipers to check the depth of cuts. Stop cutting when the leg of the calipers passes over the cut without any pressure.

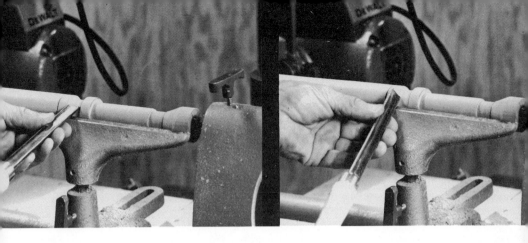

CUTTING COVES. As a rule, a gouge is used for making cove cuts. Hold the chisel in a horizontal position with the hollow part up. Start the cut at the top. Simultaneously roll and push the tool forward to the right and down toward the bottom of the cut. Start the cut from the high point in the design and work to the lowest. Then reverse the position of the tool and start the cut at the top of the other side. The bottom of each side must then be cut alternately, with the cutting chisel repeatedly shifted from right to left until the desired shape of the cove cut has been made.

CUTTING BEADS. A skew can be used to cut beads. Mark the position of each bead with a line indicating the ends and centers. Begin as you would a V cut, using the toe of the skew to start it, with the heel doing most of the cutting. You should start quite high on the cylinder at the center of the bead and turn the tool in the same arc as the bead, at the same time drawing it backhand and moving it to a vertical position. If the tool is not turned as the cut is made, the heel will dig into the next bead. When one side of the bead is complete, reverse the chisel procedure to cut the other side.

SQUARE SECTIONS. When the turning has a square section as a table leg or lamp base, the stock must be accurately centered, since any error will show at the shoulder where the round meets the square. The fingers must be kept out of the way of the flying corners. Square the ends with the skew chisel, toe down, using light cuts to prevent splintering the face of the square. Then cut the square beads, with the toe thrust in at a slight angle with the axis and the handle swung gradually to the right angle.

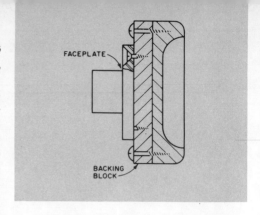

FACEPLATE

BACKING
BLOCK

MOUNTING FACEPLATE TURNING
WORK. Before attaching the faceplate, remove all surplus wood from the material by drawing a circle on it slightly larger in diameter than desired for the finished work. Cut this circle out with the saber saw. Make sure there are no checks or defects in the wood which will crack or split during the turning. Center the work accurately when screwing it to the faceplate. If the material is hardwood, drill small holes in it to start the screws. Use short, heavy flathead screws that will enter the work not more than ⅜ to ½ inch. Be sure the work is securely fastened to the faceplate and that the ends of the screws won't come in contact with the cutting chisel. When the shape of the finished piece is such that contact with the screws can't be avoided, the work must be backed up with a disc of the

same size. Bore and countersink the holes for the screws at points where they won't come in contact with the chisel. Screw this extra disc or backing plate on the work and attach it to the faceplate. Place the faceplate on the headstock spindle and tighten the setscrew. Move the tool rest so its top edge is about ⅛ inch above the center of the revolving stock; lock with wrench.

TRUING THE STOCK. With the lathe rotating at slow speed, use a square-nose, skew or gouge cutting tool to true the face. Hold it on its side with the cutting edge parallel to the front of the cylinder. Start at the center and take a scraping cut toward the outside nearest yourself. Take several cuts until the stock is the correct thickness. Hold a rule or square against the face surface and make sure it is true. Use the same tool to turn the edge until it is the correct diameter.

SIMPLE TURNING. With dividers, mark the location of the recess or bead on the face surface of the cylinder. Adjust the tool rest across the face and turn to shape, using various tools (left). For a simple recess, a round-nose tool is usually preferred. For

cutting a bead, choose a square-nose or skew. Sometimes the tool rest must be readjusted at an angle to the work to do certain kinds of turning. A spear-point chisel is often used to cut a sharp shoulder on the face of the work.

CHAPTER 8

SANDING, GRINDING, BUFFING, AND POLISHING

A comparison of power sanding with hand sanding would be like comparing a streamlined cruiser with a rowboat. Both of them will get you where you are going, but the power sander, like the cruiser, does the job a lot faster and easier.

With the radial-arm machine, you have a choice of two major types of power sanders—disc and drum. Each has its advantages and uses. But, unlike ordinary sanders, these attachments allow you to take full advantage of the maneuverability and flexibility of the radial-arm machine. Attached directly to the motor arbor, they can be tilted, swiveled, or elevated with absolute accuracy.

ABRASIVES. When choosing the proper abrasive, there are three things to consider: type of abrasive material, grit size, and type of coating.

Types of Abrasives. For power sanding there are four types of materials to choose from: flint, garnet, aluminum oxide, and silicon carbide.

Flint, the oldest of modern abrasives, is a soft, yellowish natural quartz mineral. It is inexpensive but not as efficient as other abrasives. Flint paper is good for removing old paint and for other jobs requiring quantity rather than quality.

Garnet, a rubylike gemstone, is the hardest natural abrasive. It's the paper most used in homeshops for finishing wood.

Aluminum oxide is a grayish-brown synthetic abrasive made from bauxite, coke, and iron filings in an electric furnace. It is very hard and tough and is fast becoming the most widely employed for all-around sanding applications.

Silicon carbide is another synthetic made of coke and sand and is the hardest abrasive manufactured today. But it is very brittle and can be used only in certain applications (see page 183). Silicon carbide paper is dark gray to black.

Grit size is determined by the number of grains which, end to end, equal 1 inch. Until recently, grain sizes were referred to by a complicated numbering system. To simplify the system, many manufacturers now label their papers as fine, medium, coarse, etc. The table on page 184 lists the numbers and equivalent names.

Type of Coating. There are two types of coating—closed and open. Closed-coat papers have tightly packed abrasive grains that cover the entire surface. The grains on open-coat papers cover 50 to 70 percent of the surface, leaving open spaces between the grains.

Closed-coat papers are durable and fast cutting, but have the disadvantage of clogging under certain conditions. Open-coated abrasives aren't as durable, but they are useful for finishing certain surfaces such as soft or gummy woods, paint and other finishes, and soft metals and plastics where the abrasive dust tends to clog the disc or drum.

Discs are available cut to size, while the drum's sleeve can be purchased cut to size or made from 9 by 11 inch sheets (see page 97).

BASIC RULES OF POWER SANDING:

■ Always select the grade of abrasive carefully for the job you want. See Abrasive Selection Chart, page 183.

■ Always sand with the grain of the wood.

■ Do all the cutting operations before sanding. Except for special jobs, the sander is designed to finish the surface of the work, not to shape it.

■ Apply enough pressure to complete the work. The tendency of the beginner is to press too hard and attempt too big a pass, thus cutting scratches in the surface.

■ Clean off the abrasive paper or cloth with a brush at frequent intervals.

■ Always sand surfaces square. The tendency in sanding is to round all edges and surfaces. Don't spoil the accuracy of your work by careless sanding.

■ "Break" all edges slightly to prevent splintering. The corners should be rounded to about the diameter of the lead in a pencil.

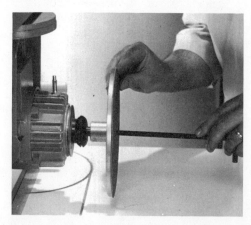

MOUNTING THE DISC SANDER. Remove the safety guard, arbor nut, cutting tool, and the arbor collars from the motor shaft. Then replace arbor collars, the disc plate on the shaft, and tighten counterclockwise with your hand. Hold the shaft with a hex wrench while tightening the disc plate.

APPLYING ABRASIVE DISC. The new abrasive discs have pressure sensative backs, making it unnecessary to use glue. Simply peel the backing from the disc, lay it on the metal plate, and smooth it out. It's easy to remove an old disc—just peel it off the metal plate. Best results will be achieved if the plate is thoroughly cleaned before applying a new disc.

FREEHAND SANDING. Work on the disc sander is usually done freehand. It is held flat on the auxiliary table (see page 20) and projected into the sanding disc. A smooth light feed should be practiced. Remember that abrasive particles are cutting teeth, they can only remove so much material. Avoid heavy pressure, it may cause the work and paper to burn. The paper may become clogged and useless long before it should. Also, with a disc sander it is important to do the sanding on the "down" side of the disc.

BUTT SANDING. Place the motor in the crosscut position and set the auxiliary table jig in place of the guide fence. With the material tight against the fence of the auxiliary table and making contact with the disc, pull the motor past the material in the same manner as when cross-cutting. If you are doing fine butt sanding, swing the motor 1° to 3° to the left for the down-rotation operation.

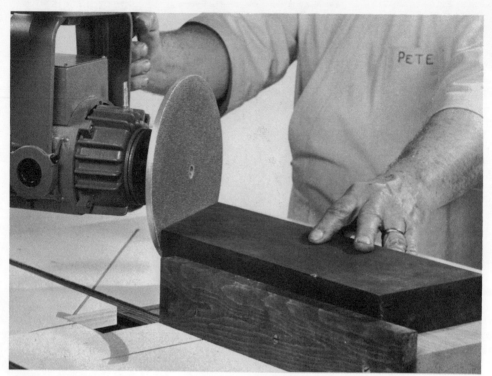

MITER SANDING. With the motor in the crosscut position, locate the arm at the desired miter angle and replace the guide fence with the auxiliary table. Position your material on the table so it contacts the abrasive; pull the motor across the miter end of the board. If finer sanding is required, swivel the motor 1° to 3° to the left.

DOUBLE MITER SANDING. To sand compound angle work, swing the arm to the desired miter angle and place the motor at the proper angle of bevel. Then, set the precut stock on the auxiliary table and pull the disc across the board. When double miter sanding, it's wise to use the tool guard.

SANDING CIRCLES. You can sand circles and curves to accurate size and true radius on a disc sander if you use the jig illustrated on page 81. Start the job with a perfectly square board and find the exact center by using the diagonal method. Then cut to the approximate circumference of the circle on the saber saw or as described on page 36. Place the stock to be sanded on the center pin of the sliding strip of the jig and set the motor in the crosscut position. Lower the motor to the proper height and lock it in place directly in front of the jig. Turn on the machine and slowly rotate the stock clockwise on the center pin (moving it closer to the disc from time to time) until it is perfectly round and uniformly smooth.

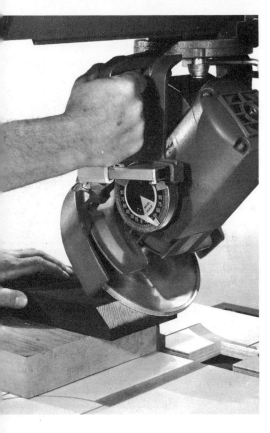

BEVEL SANDING. With the arm in the crosscut position, place the motor at the desired angle of bevel and locate the auxiliary table in place of the guide fence. Position your stock on the jig so it contacts the sander. Pull the disc across the beveled end of the board. As in butt sanding, swinging the motor 1° to 3° to the left will produce a finer job.

ROUNDING CORNERS. The sanding of round corners is similar to circular work in that the edge being worked is part of a true circle. This can be done freehand by sweeping the corner of the work across the face of the sanding disc two or three times until the desired curve is obtained. The motor is placed in the crosscut position and locked into place with the rip lock.

material above the surface of the table, the simple auxiliary table used for horizontal sawing (see page 26) is ideal. Place the auxiliary jig on the edge of the table. Then position the motor and lock it in place with the rip clamp. You can place the material to be sanded on the auxiliary table against its fence and push the material past the disc. If fine sanding is desired, swivel the motor 1° to 3° to the left so the material contacts the disc on the down rotation only.

STRAIGHTEDGE SANDING. Swing the radial arm 60° to the left and place the motor so the front of the disc sander is parallel to and along the guide fence. This is done by adjusting the swivel-clamp handle and the swivel-latch assembly. To raise the

RAISED-PANEL SANDING. Another job on which the radial-arm disc sander is especially effective is finishing the beveled edges of a raised panel. This is difficult to do by hand-sanding, but the setup shown here does the trick in a professional manner. Care, however, must be taken in locating the disc in relation to the bevel.

SURFACE SANDING. To position the machine for general surfacing, elevate the radial arm until the motor with the disc attached can be tilted to the vertical position. Then move the motor along the arm until the disc is directly above the path the material will follow along the guide fence, and lock it in position with the rip clamp. Place your stock on the table and lower the arm until the disc fits snugly against the top surface of the board. Then push the board from right to left along the fence. For this sanding operation, use the tool guard.

MOUNTING THE DRUM SANDER. To mount either the 1- or 2½-inch drum sander, place both arbor collars and the arbor nut on the arbor. Tighten the arbor nut against the collars. Use the wrench to hold the arbor nut, and with the left hand, thread on the drum sander as tightly as possible.

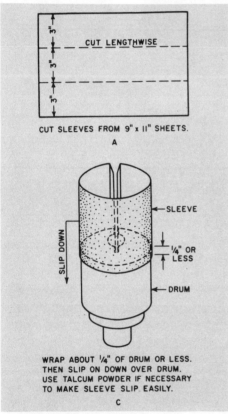

CUT SLEEVES FROM 9" x 11" SHEETS.

A

WRAP ABOUT ¼" OF DRUM OR LESS. THEN SLIP ON DOWN OVER DRUM. USE TALCUM POWDER IF NECESSARY TO MAKE SLEEVE SLIP EASILY.

C

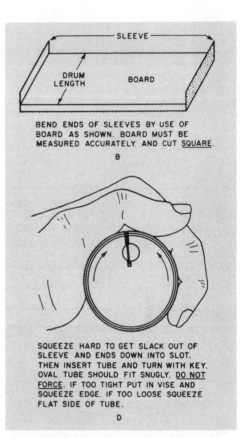

BEND ENDS OF SLEEVES BY USE OF BOARD AS SHOWN. BOARD MUST BE MEASURED ACCURATELY AND CUT SQUARE.

B

SQUEEZE HARD TO GET SLACK OUT OF SLEEVE AND ENDS DOWN INTO SLOT. THEN INSERT TUBE AND TURN WITH KEY. OVAL TUBE SHOULD FIT SNUGLY. DO NOT FORCE. IF TOO TIGHT PUT IN VISE AND SQUEEZE EDGE. IF TOO LOOSE SQUEEZE FLAT SIDE OF TUBE.

D

REPLACING SANDPAPER SLEEVE. To replace the sleeve on your drum sander, use a ready-cut one or make a new sleeve by cutting a 9- by 11-inch sheet of sandpaper of the proper grit into three 3- by 11-inch strips by tearing it against a metal straightedge or hacksaw blade. (Never cut the sandpaper with scissors or knife, as this will damage the cutting edge of the tool.) Bend the ends of the sleeves by the use of a board as shown. The board must be measured accurately and cut square. Wrap the sleeve around the drum approximately ¼-inch down on it and slide the ends in the slot. Slip the sleeve over the drum. A little talcum powder on the soft rubber drum will make the sleeve slip on more easily. Squeeze hard to take the slack out of the sleeve and push the ends down into the slot. Then insert the tube that comes with the drum and turn it with a key. The oval tube should fit snugly; don't force it. If it is too tight, put it in a vise and squeeze the edge; if too loose, squeeze the flat side of the tube.

FREEHAND SANDING. With the radial arm raised to its maximum height, place the motor in the vertical position and locate it on the arm so that the drum is centered over the shaper slot on the table. Tighten the rip clamp and lower the arm so the entire edge of the stock being finished will come in contact with the abrasive. Move the work past the drum from right to left.

INTERNAL SANDING. Raise the arm so the material can be inserted under the drum and then lower it back into position. Proceed to move the work around as described for freehand sanding. But, remember that when using a drum sander, the material being finished should be kept constantly in motion to prevent overheating and scorching the wood.

STRAIGHT SANDING. Straight work usually requires a guide fence or the use of the jointer fence. (With the latter, there should be a $1/64$ inch offset between the infeed and outfeed edges.) With the motor at the rear, bring the sander forward into the shaper slot on the table. Locate the sander so its leading edge is in a straight line with the outfeed side of the fence and tighten the rip clamp on the radial arm. Place the material against the infeed side of the fence, start the motor, and push the stock past the sander. Be sure to keep the work moving at a uniform rate, from right to left, past the drum. If the work is stopped at any point while in contact with the rotating drum, it may be scored or burned. Uneven feed can produce scoring at intervals along the length of the stock.

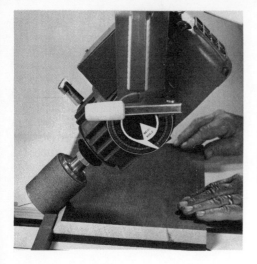

BEVEL SANDING. With the arm in the crosscut position, turn the yoke to the in-rip position, and place the motor at the desired angle of bevel as shown. Then feed the precut stock past the drum sander at a uniform speed.

SURFACE SANDING NARROW BOARDS. With the motor raised to its full extent, set the shaft in a horizontal position. Place the material tight against the fence, and lower the radial arm until the abrasive hits the start of the stock. Withdraw the stock, turn on the motor, and *feed the work against the rotation of the drum.* If smoother work is desired, lower the arm a quarter turn at a time.

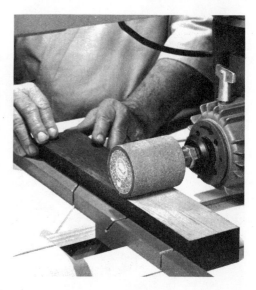

SURFACE SANDING WIDE BOARDS. Wider boards—up to twice the width of the paper—may be handled in the same manner except that a second pass will have to be made with the sander at the same height. Remember —in any surface sanding operation, don't attempt too deep a bite in one pass. Two or more passes will result in a better job.

SANDING RABBETS. The inside corners of rabbets and similar cuts can be done easily with the drum sander. The rabbeted stock is put against the guide fence, with the drum set to fit in the corner. Feed the work forward, past the drum, to make the cut. For operations like this, the sleeve should be mounted so it projects about $1/32$ inch beyond the bottom of the drum, allowing the inside corner to be finished cleanly.

CONCAVE SANDING. One problem the craftsman frequently encounters is fitting a leg to a round column. As shown here, the drum sander on the radial-arm machine can solve the problem. The $2\frac{1}{2}$-inch drum is generally used for this task since it represents most closely the average diameter of the work. An auxiliary table is needed to bring the center of the drum in line with the center of the leg on which the concave surface is to be shaped.

GRINDING, BUFFING, AND POLISHING.

The versatility of the radial-arm machine makes it possible to convert to a grinder, wire brush, or buffer as quickly as you can change a blade.

The most important use of the grinding wheel is to sharpen tools. Sharp tools aid accuracy, reduce finishing operations and accidents. The radial-arm grinder can be used for sharpening plane blades, wood chisels, lathe tools, screwdrivers, and drills.

For most uses, the grinder is generally fitted with either a medium-grain or a fine-grain abrasive wheel. The medium wheel should be used on metal surfaces where smoothness is not too important. The fine wheel is generally used when close tolerance is required or for sharpening. When a considerable amount of metal is to be removed or when a deep cut is to be made, the work can be speeded by using the medium wheel first and then finishing with the fine wheel. Two types of wheels are suitable for the radial-arm machine—cup wheels and disc wheels.

For most sharpening operations, the motor shaft should be horizontal and swung to the left (standard cross-cut position). In this way, the grinding wheel will run toward you, which will help to eliminate the formation of a wire edge.

Sparks given off by a grinding wheel indicate different grades of steel or iron. High-carbon tool steel creates bright white sparks which travel only a short distance from the wheel. Wrought iron gives off a reddish-yellow spark which travels quite a distance. Cold-rolled steel and mild steel fall somewhere between these two. High-speed steel produces a bright yellow spark that stops abruptly a few inches from the wheel.

The grinder and wire brush must be handled with care, and the following general safety precautions should be kept in mind when using these attachments.

■ Always wear goggles when grinding or wire brushing and be sure they cover the eyes properly.

■ Stand to one side of the wheel when the machine is started.

■ Let the wheel warm up before using it heavily; feed the work gradually. Using too much pressure or striking the wheel suddenly may cause it to break.

■ Keep the tool-rest approximately 1/8 inch from the grinding wheel. Too much clearance may cause the piece being sharpened to jam the wheel and break it.

■ Don't set the tool rest while the wheel, brush, or buffer is turning. Wait for the motor to stop after the power has been shut off. Don't attempt to stop the wheel with your hands.

MOUNTING THE WHEEL AND THE GUARD. To mount any of the three wheels—grinder, wire brush, or buffer—all you have to do is remove the safety guard, arbor nut, cutting device, and arbor collars. Replace one collar, place the desired wheel on the shaft, followed by the other arbor collar, and tighten them on the shaft with the arbor nut (left). The wheel guard is mounted in the same manner as the other machine safety guards. The chip and spark deflectors for the grinding wheel can very easily be interchanged without removing the entire guard unit so that either the cup wheel or the larger diameter wheels can be used. You'll note (right) that the guard has a built-in tool rest eliminating the need for a special tool-rest jig.

WIRE-BRUSH OPERATION. The wire wheel may be used to give a beautiful brushed effect on soft-metal projects. It may be used also for removing dirt, grease, or oxide from the surface of metal in preparation for brazing or soldering. It will also remove rust and corrosion in preparation for refinishing or repainting. You can usually hold the work against the brush by hand. Take it easy; do not force the work into the wire brush as it will scratch the metal. If metal surfaces should become scratched when wire brushing, buffing will remove them. Always use the guard which is provided with the wire brush attachment.

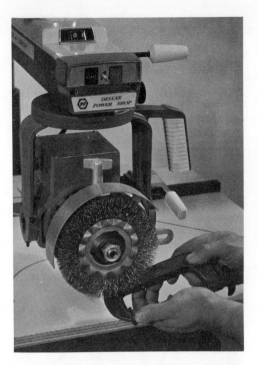

SHARPENING EDGED TOOLS. When grinding an edged tool, adjust the tool rest so the bevel side of the iron rests on the wheel to produce the proper angle. Move the blade from side to side, grinding until a burr appears on the upper edge. Dip it in water often to cool. To remove the burr, use either an aluminum oxide or a silicon carbide oilstone. The stone should be well oiled—use thin oil or kerosene—so that the metal particles will not become embedded in the stone. The burr is removed by turning the tool on its flat side and lightly stroking it diagonally backward and forward. Repeat the honing process until the burr disappears. Avoid any bevel on this side.

BUFFING OPERATION. A high polish may be given to lacquered, painted and varnished wood surfaces, plastics, ivory, bone, copper, pewter, brass, aluminum, etc., on the radial–arm machine by the use of a buffing or polishing wheel. (The proper polishing compounds, and the materials they are recommended for, are listed on page 177.) To charge the wheel, the polishing compound is held against the spinning wheel. Friction softens the material which then adheres to the cloth wheel. All polishing or buffing work should be done on the lower quarter of the wheel, as shown. Since the wheel should be clean for the application of each compound, use benzine or lacquer thinner to remove any film of the compound that remains.

GRINDER-BUFFER WHEEL. Some jobs will require more metal removal than can be done by buffing. A solid grinding wheel will do this, of course, but it cannot follow contours. However, you can make a wheel for flexible grinding. Take a buffer wheel and roll it in good liquid glue which has been poured on wax paper. Coat the face uniformly with the glue and smooth the coating with your fingers or a stick. Hang the buffer on a nail to dry for 12 to 24 hours. After it has dried, place the wheel on the motor shaft and mark an arrow on the side of the wheel to show the direction of rotation (always be sure to put it back on the shaft the same way). Run the wheel and sand its face lightly with coarse or medium sandpaper to smooth the surface. Roll the wheel in the glue preparation again and then roll it in a flat pile of abrasive which you have spread out on the waxed paper. Let the weight of the wheel provide the pressure. Allow an hour for drying. Repeat the treatment and then allow 12 to 24 hours to dry. The following day, scrape any loose grains from the sides of the wheel and crack the face by flexing it with your thumb or pressing it with a blunt tool. The face should now have hundreds of small cracks. Mount the wheel on the motor shaft and break it in by polishing a piece of scrap metal lightly. Be very careful of this wheel, as it cuts fairly rapidly.

CHAPTER 9

A HOME FOR THE RADIAL-ARM MACHINE

The radial-arm machine is the heart of a home workshop. The reason, as you have learned from the previous chapters, is that it can perform the work of a circular saw, saber saw, shaper, disc and drum sander, router, grinder, and horizontal borer—and even a lathe.

The things to consider in planning a home for your radial-arm machine are: source of electricity, sawdust disposal, treatment of walls and floors, lighting, built-in features, heating, and layout. The last item—layout of the radial-arm machine—is often assumed to cover the whole subject, but as a matter of fact, floor plans are useful only in giving the beginner a general idea of the space required. The best plan is the one that allows for flexibility and planned growth. Nothing is more discouraging than trying to work in cramped quarters. You'll save time and headaches, and do better work, if you begin by considering the size of your shop. The radial-arm machine is ideal for restricted areas because of its exceptional versatility. Unlike a table saw, the radial-arm machine doesn't require accessibility from all sides. In other words, you can use a rather compact one-wall arrangement, if you desire.

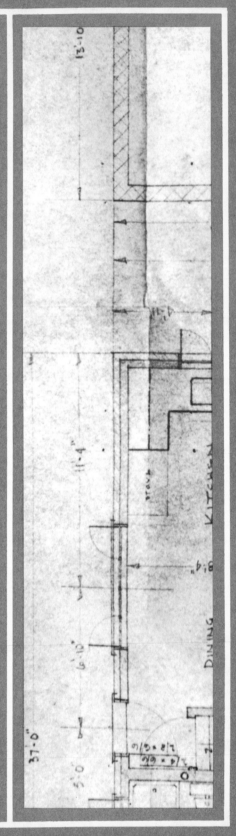

A shop can be set up in your basement, attic, or garage. In the attic the machine can be placed under the eaves, using space that would otherwise be wasted. The back wall of a garage can also be used. A compact radial-arm machine can even find a home in an apartment. But, when finding a spot for the radial-arm machine, adequate space should be allowed for handling materials. About 10 feet on either side will allow for most ripping and handling of long boards. Two feet of operating area is all that is required at the front of the machine. Table extensions are preferred for supporting long work and should be solid or made of wood with metal rollers to help in conveying stock past the blade.

A new concept in planning your workshop for flexibility and growth is illustrated at the end of this chapter by the home shops developed for the "House of Good Taste" exhibit at the 1964-65 New York World's Fair.

When considering your shop location, remember this: Is it accessible? This applies not only to you, but to the materials that must be brought in and the completed projects that will be taken out. You've heard the story about the fellow who built a beautiful boat in his basement and then had to tear down the house to get it out. Consider the size of the doorway in relation to your projects. A 3-foot minimum opening is best, though you may feel you can get by with a 2½-foot opening. Avoid narrow, twisting stairs and halls, if possible.

Good artificial light is essential, especially if you do most of your work at night. Lighting can be direct or indirect, incandescent or fluorescent. Incandescent light, with silvered bulbs that can be pulled down, is best for close work. Of course, the more natural light you can get without shadows, the better. To improve the natural light, many home craftsmen have replaced old cellar windows with larger ones.

In planning your workshop it is well to remember that your radial-arm machine must have a solid base. This may take one of several different forms: leg stands, steel cabinets, or built-in bench units.

STEEL CABINET. One of newest accessories for a radial-arm machine is the steel cabinet shown here. This cabinet provides plenty of storage for accessories and tools as well as an excellent base for the machine.

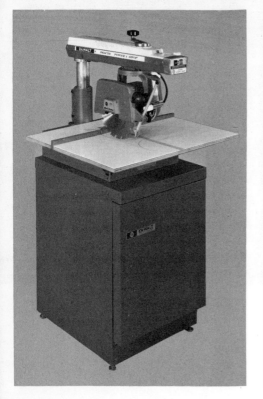

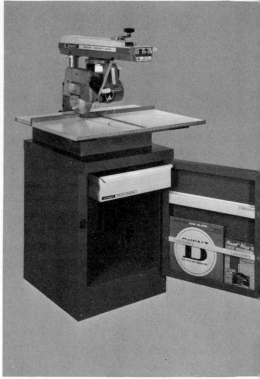

LEG STAND. A leg stand makes a solid base, especially for the light-weight, compact home shop unit shown. While this compact radial-arm machine weighs only 78 pounds, it performs the multi-purpose operations of more deluxe units.

The metal stand supporting the unit can be assembled easily, can be built into a workbench or fitted with extensions for support of long material.

The metal ribs at the bottom not only provide reinforcement, but also give solid support for a storage shelf.

An ambitious craftsman can go one step further by closing in the sides, thus making a full storage cabinet or a series of shelves or compartments for accessories and other tools.

BUILT-IN WORKBENCH. The ideal arrangement for your machine is to build it into, and make it part of, the workbench itself. The plan shown here features a complete shop in itself—permitting maximum storage and operational flexibility because of its two uses in one. The workbench not only houses the radial-arm machine, but also serves as a work table for other uses when the radial-arm is swung back against the tool board in the out-of-the-way position. Handy drawers and doors, and a pegboard attached to the back of the workbench offer ideal storage for the machine's accessories and hand tools. The space under the workbench is an excellent storage area for spare lumber and unfinished parts. Full construction details are given and the workbench is easy to complete. Actually, it can easily be your first project with the radial-arm machine. While building the bench, you can operate the machine on a pair of saw-horses.

MATERIAL LIST
Note - All sizes in USE COLUMN are finish sizes

BUY	USE	PART	NO. REQUIRED
	PINE		
	3/4 x 1-1/8 x 27-3/4	(1)	2
2 pc. 1" x 2" x 12'	3/4 x 1-3/8 x 50-1/4	(S)	1
	3/4 x 1-3/8 x 68-1/4	(R)	1
	3/4 x 1-3/8 x 18	(RR)	2
	3/4 x 1-1/2 x 16-5/8	(L)	2
	3/4 x 2 x 4-7/8	(U)	1
	3/4 x 2 x 9	(V)	1
1 px. 1" x 3" x 7'	3/4 x 2 x 15-1/4	(W)	1
	3/4 x 2 x 18	(T)	2
	3/4 x 2-1/4 x 7-3/8	(F)	1
1 pc. 2" x 2" x 5'	1-1/8 x 1-1/4 x 27-3/4	(M)	1
	1-1/8 x 1-3/4 x 27-3/4	(N)	1
	FIR		
1 pc. 1-1/2" x 1-1/2" x 4'	1" x 1" x 6"	Handles	6
1 pc. 2" x 4" x 10'	1-5/8 x 3-5/8 x 20-1/2	(G)	2
	1-5/8 x 3-5/8 x 35-1/4	(C)	1
	1-5/8 x 3-5/8 x 35-1/4	(D)	1
2 pc. 4" x 4" x 6'	3-5/8 x 3-5/8 33-1/2	(O) (P)	4

U.S. PLYWOOD MATERIAL
(See Cutting Diagrams for details)

1 pc. 1/4" x 3' x 4'	*Weldwood ®Fir Plywood
1 pc. 1/2" x 4' x 8'	*Weldwood ®Fir Plywood
1 pc. 3/4" x 4' x 6'	*Weldwood ®Fir Plywood
1 pc. 3/4" x 4' x 6'	*Weldwood Duraply ®

MISCELLANEOUS

2" Angle Brackets	6
1" Angle Brackets	4
3/8" Offset Cabinet Hinges	6
Friction Catches	2
Wood Screws	
Nails	

*Weldwood ® is a registered trade mark for the products made by the United States Plywood Corporation . . . ask for them at your lumber dealer's.

CUTTING DIAGRAMS

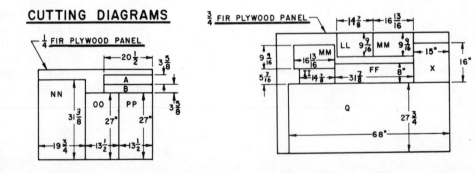

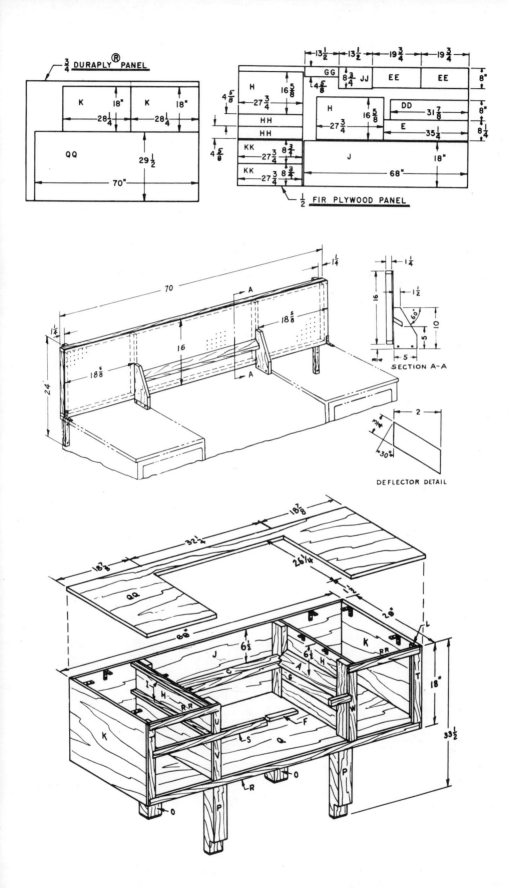

¾ DURAPLY® PANEL

K 18" K 18"
28¼ 28¼

QQ 29½

70"

13½ 13½ 19¾ 19¾

GG 8¾ JJ EE EE 8"
H 16⅝ 4⅝
4⅝ 27¾

HH
HH

H 16⅝ DD 31⅞ 8"
27¾ E 35¼ 8¼

KK 8¾
4⅝ 27¾
KK 8¾ J 68" 18"
27¾

½ FIR PLYWOOD PANEL

70
1¼
1¼
18⅝
16
18⅝
24

A
A

SECTION A-A
1¼
1½
16
60°
10
5
5

DEFLECTOR DETAIL
2
¾
30°

18⅞
32¼
18⅞
26¼
QQ

6½
J
C
H
A
G
I
H
R R
U
L S
V
Q
O
R
K
K
R R
L
T
W
F
P
O
P
2⌀
6½
18"
33½

111

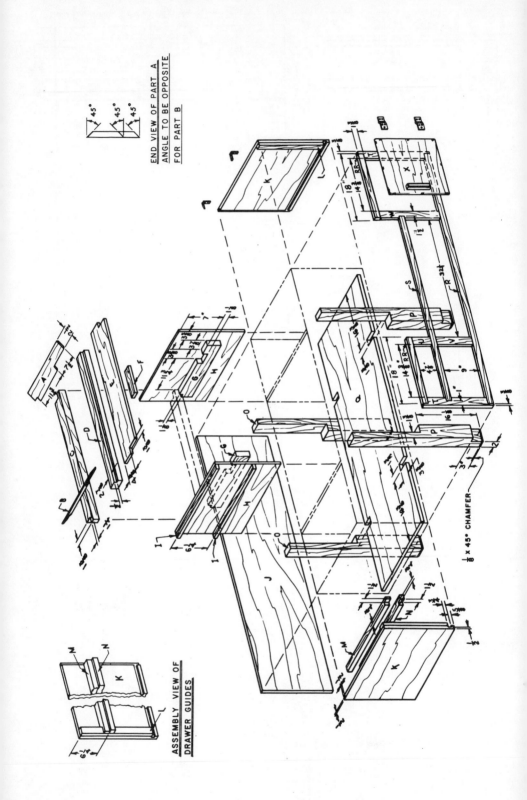

END VIEW OF PART A
ANGLE TO BE OPPOSITE
FOR PART B

ASSEMBLY VIEW OF
DRAWER GUIDES

⅛ × 45° CHAMFER

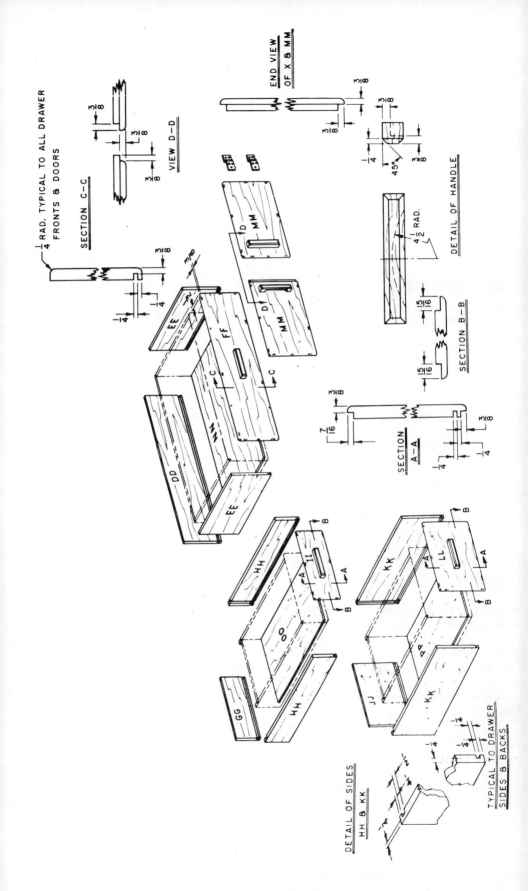

SECTION C–C

VIEW D–D

END VIEW
OF X & MM

¼ RAD. TYPICAL TO ALL DRAWER
FRONTS & DOORS

DETAIL OF HANDLE

4½ RAD.

SECTION B–B

SECTION A–A

DETAIL OF SIDES
HH & KK

TYPICAL TO DRAWER
SIDES & BACKS

113

PLANNING FOR GROWTH. In the "House of Good Taste" exhibit at the 1964-65 New York World's Fair, a new concept of shop planning was unveiled by Black & Decker. This "building block" plan affords complete interchangeability and solves the problem of costly structural alterations as your shop expands. Each house in the exhibit has a complete tool shop center to match the needs of its owner. Each shop is equipped with the latest Black & Decker portable and radial-arm power tools and accessories.

The key to the shop designs is the *modular unit.* Starting with a small basic shop for the new home owner who needs minimum maintenance and repair equipment, more modules are added for the larger center, giving the seasoned home craftsman and full-fledged hobbyist a complete selection of professional power tool equipment. All shops include ample shelf, drawer, and pegboard-panel storage space for hand tools, nuts and bolts, paint supplies, saw horses, and other usual shop accessories.

YOUR HOME MAINTENANCE HEADQUARTERS. The basic shop, designed by experts and equipped with power tools and accessories, consists of five basic modules—including a workbench area with a unique revolving "Lazy Susan," storage cabinets, and a wall rack for convenient placement of power tools. Each workbench unit is 34-inches high, with ¼-inch Tempered Hardboard screwed to two pieces of ¾-inch fir plywood glued together to form the working surface. This surface will withstand the hard usage it will receive. The outstanding features of this shop include a pegboard rack for hand tools, a wall-hung storage unit for portable power tools including sander, drill, circular and saber saws, and a saw horse storage cabinet. One storage compartment houses a portable tote box fitted to hold pegboard partitions for hand tools. Its 23-inch height allows it to double as a saw horse. This practical, easy-to-build shop holds just the right assortment of drills, saws, and sanders for complete home maintenance. The moderately-priced power tools used to equip this shop are in the "Utility" range and include a ¼-inch electric drill with attachments, a circular saw, a jig saw, and a finishing sander. All of these units have appropriate accessories. There are also horizontal and vertical drill stands for bench use. Chapter 14 outlines the basic uses of these power tools.

THE MASTER SHOP. This is the ultimate shop for the expert home mechanic and accomplished hobbyist. In addition, it truly offers a world of home shop wonders to benefit the entire family. The modular units used in the basic shop are regrouped and new units are added, including a tool turret and a rolling lumber rack for storing odds and ends of material.

Space is provided for a multi-purpose DeWalt unit. Power tools are of the "Professional" grade, and include a 3/8-inch electric drill, a router-plane kit, a jig saw, and a finishing sander. Cordless equipment includes the 1/4-inch electric drill and a cordless hedge trimmer. A 6-inch bench grinder completes the power tool equipment of the shop.

PORTABLE TOOL BOARDS. The last word in efficient space-saving. Detachable pegboard cabinet doors store hand tools in easy reach without stretching. Plastic or metal hooks lock into perforations. Located just above the work surface, where tools can easily be replaced after use, these storage-doors save time by keeping the shop well-organized.

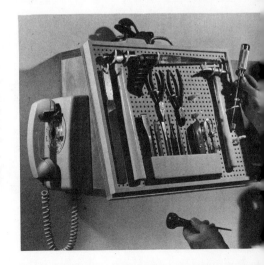

EXTRA STORAGE SPACE. Behind the tool boards, storage shelves keep small parts and other supplies within arm's reach. The tool board is hinged at the top, can't swing open to collide with the lumber you're handling—or with your head.

COMPLETE SHOP. A complete shop means using not only modern tools and equipment, but providing for proper lighting, adequate ventilation, and efficient cleaning equipment. Clean tools and work area lead to greater safety and enjoyment in the shop. A modern built-in B&D vacuum cleaning system can provide noiseless, dustless cleaning for the shop floor, workbench, or tools, just as it can for other rooms throughout the house.

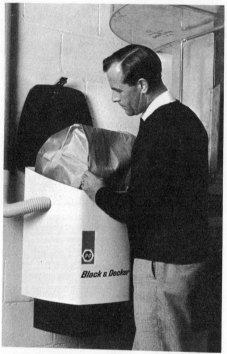

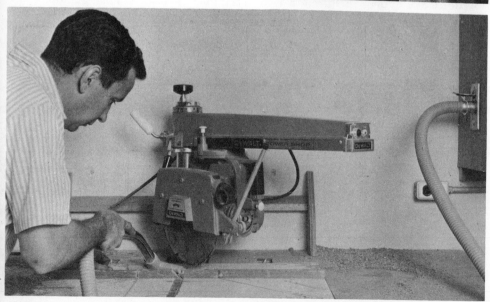

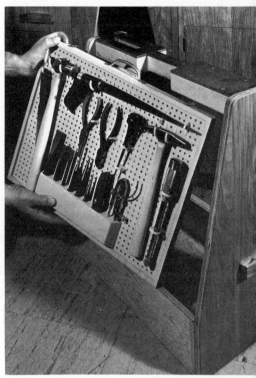

BASE-UNIT BONUS. Fitted snugly into one of the modular bench units is an up-to-date version of the carpenter's carryall for power or hand tools. Its height makes for easier handling and allows it to double as a saw horse.

EXTRA FLEXIBILITY. Carrying out the scheme of interchangeable units, the tote box can be fitted with any two of the tool boards that can be carried alone. Use the bottom of the box to carry nails, screws, glue, etc., and end rummaging to find the tool you want.

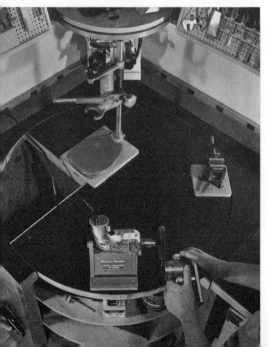

LAZY SUSAN. Revolving workbench-cabinet unit combines four work areas in one. Interchangeable tools and jigs lock into slots on turntable; a quarter-turn brings each to the front. This 41-inch wide unit replaces 24 square feet of work and storage space.

CORNER RACK. This unit shrinks the wall space needed to store four portable power tools — drill, finishing sander, circular saw, and saber saw. Eye-level location is out of the way but handy. Fitted openings protect blades and bits.

ROLL-AROUND RADIAL SAW. Fifteen tools in one—plus mobility. Slide-out handle and wheels at the back allow this unit to operate like a wheelbarrow without losing stability. The unit can fit between other bench units for maximum work surface.

ROLLING LUMBER RACK. This easy-to-build, free-wheeling unit keeps useful scraps from underfoot and saves more wall space. Interior partitions make for easy sorting.

CHAPTER 10

WOODWORKING TECHNIQUES

To complete any project successfully you must have some knowledge of fastenings, joint construction, hardware installation and, of course, finishing. It is impossible, in a book of this size, to give complete details on these subjects. Several excellent books are available at your local book store or library that cover these procedures in more detail than we will be able to. However, the following information will certainly help you turn out better work in your home shop.

BASIC PROCEDURES: In all woodworking projects you should follow these six major procedures:

■ Lay out the project by measuring, diagramming, and estimating the quantity of materials needed.

■ Mark the materials for length, width, and shape. Use a well-sharpened pencil, knife, or stylus for marking out lines. Be sure the point of the pencil is as close to the edge of the rule or square as possible. The thickness of a blunt pencil point can often mean the difference between a good fit and a poor one.

■ Cut the material to the exact size required. Always make your cut on the outside, or waste side, of the line

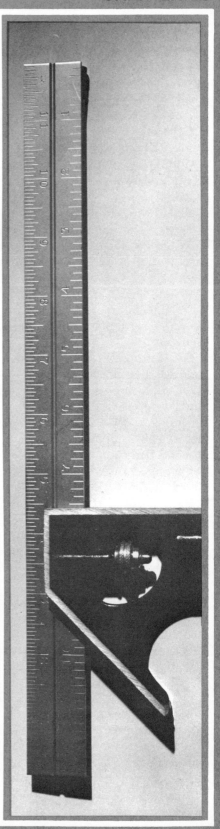

marked on the board. The blade of the saw has some thickness, and if you saw on the finish side of the line or along the line itself, you may find that in spite of your accuracy in measuring, the material is too short.

■ Join the cut parts into the desired assembly by nailing, screwing, or gluing and by using the most appropriate of the wide variety of joints available.

■ Prepare the surface for finishing.

■ Apply the finish material selected to give the project its final appearance.

To get the best results from any project, there are certain other fundamental principles that must be followed:

■ Be accurate when taking measurements and laying out work.

■ Lay out the job clearly by marking the different pieces—front, back, side, etc. Also mark all companion pieces where joints appear as 1 and 1, 2 and 2, etc.

■ Plan ahead as each step is completed.

■ Be orderly and neat. Take pride in turning out a fine job.

■ Use only the best materials. The difference in cost between good and cheap materials is small; it pays to buy the best.

■ All lumber must be squared. Find any deviation from a right angle, straight line, or plane surface, and true it before proceeding with the actual work. (See page 65 for details of this operation.)

■ Joints must be made to fit together; never make them too loose or too tight. Remember, your finished item is only as strong as its weakest joint.

■ Wherever possible, duplicate pieces should be laid out and cut at the same time.

■ Keep all tools in good condition. A sharp blade or cutter makes work easier, safer, and more accurate. Unless you have had experience in sharpening saw blades, it is best to have this work done by a professional. Your local hardware or lumber dealer will usually do this for you.

FASTENINGS. Wood projects can be held together or fastened by nails, screws, glue, or a combination of any of these. But, regardless of the fastener employed, three basic principles must be considered:

1. Fasteners must be strong enough to support both external and internal stresses.

2. Fasteners must be placed so as to overcome any tendency of the wood to bend, belly, or buckle.

3. Fasteners must be of a type to compensate for any potential movement. Movement must be anticipated where there are extreme fluctuations in moisture content or where panels are fastened to supporting members of different materials.

NAILING. A nail must be properly selected for the work it is to do so that it won't split the wood or distort the fibers. The types of nail that distorts the fibers of the wood the least will have the greatest holding power. For finishing work, casing nails hold better than finish nails. Nailheads can be driven flush or slightly set with a nail set and filled with wood filler, spackle, or putty. When this is done, the nail holes will be almost invisible and the panels will be ready for finishing. If appearance isn't important, box or common nails should be used. Spiral or ring-barbed nails give extra holding power. For exterior work, use hot-dipped zinc-coated nails to avoid rust.

HOLDING WITH SCREWS. Screws have much greater holding power than nails. Moreover, screws can be removed and replaced without damaging the pieces. Holes of slightly smaller diameter than the screws should be drilled first. It also helps to soap the screws. Sizes given here are minimums; use longer screws when work permits. Screws should be countersunk and the holes filled with wood filler, dough, or surfacing putty. Apply the filler so it is slightly higher than the surface of the wood and sand it level when dry.

It is often desirable to cover the head of the screw with a wood plug that matches the type of wood used. With a plug cutter, cut a small disc that will cover the head of the screw (plug cutters are available in various sizes). A hole $3/8$ inch in diameter is satisfactory for most screws. Bore the hole $3/16$ inch deep, and drive the head of the screw to the bottom of the hole. Cut the plug from a thin piece of the same kind of wood, match the grain as nearly as possible, and glue the plug into the hole so that it follows the grain of the wood.

GLUING. In furniture construction, gluing is the most common joining method. Choose your glue from the Glue Chart on page 182.

Before starting to assemble any project, inspect each piece to be sure all sandpapering has been completed. Put all the pieces together without glue to make sure the joints come together as they should and are square and true. Mark all companion pieces, where joints appear, as 1 and 1, 2 and 2, etc., and indicate front right, front left, etc., with a soft pencil. Once this is done, the different pieces will fit together as they should for the actual gluing without further adjustment; this is important since the assembly period (the time between spreading the glue and appli-

cation of pressure) should not exceed fifteen minutes. The clamp should also be set to the correct size beforehand to facilitate the final gluing. Now put all hand screws and clamps in position (no glue yet) ; remember to put scrap blocks of wood under the clamps so they won't bruise the surfaces. Inspect the work once more, for it is not too late to trim a joint a little or make a necessary alteration. Planning pays off in assembly, just as in cutting. Frequently, you can break down complicated projects into subassemblies that are easier to handle and make joints more accessible.

Apply glue with a brush or stick to only one of the surfaces to be bonded (except when using contact cement). Use plenty of glue; do not starve the joint. End grain absorbs glue quickly, so it is best to apply a preliminary coat, allow it to soak for a few minutes, and then apply another coat. Gluing must be done in a warm, dry, draft-free room. Apply clamps with full jaw length in contact, and make sure jaws are parallel. Otherwise, pressure is applied to only part of the joint. Nails, screws, or other fasteners may also be used as temporary clamps. After the clamps have been applied, test the job for squareness. Wipe off excess glue, since some glues stain wood and make it difficult to achieve a good finish. It helps to throw sawdust over the glue as it oozes out of the joint; the sawdust absorbs the moisture of the glue and makes it easier to peel off the excess. Never wash off excess glue with water. Water coats the wood with a thin layer of glue which may show when it dries and can also make the wood swell, which is very undesirable. The work must be held together under pressure until the glue is hard, which will vary from $1\frac{1}{2}$ to 16 hours, depending on the temperature and type of glue.

dry. Apply glue to the mitered ends and hold them together with the clamps so they are aligned. After the glue has set, remove the clamps, pry the blocks away, and sand off the paper.

When the glue is dry, remove the clamps and start the final cleaning job. Using a sharp chisel, hold the tool with the bevel side up and cut carefully, across the grain where possible, to remove all traces of glue. Give a final sandpapering to all parts by using first fine and then very fine sandpaper.

DOWELING. Many types of joints— miter, edge, butt, and mortise and tenon—are greatly strengthened by installing dowels. Dowels are hardwood rods—generally maple or birch —and are available in diameters from $\frac{1}{8}$ to 3 inches, with either a plain or grooved surface. The latter allows the glue to run more freely into the joint. (You can groove your own dowel sticks, see page 82.)

In selecting the size of dowel rod to use, a general rule is that the diameter should be no more than half the thickness of the stock. The depth of the hole will vary with the type of joint. The length of the dowel rod should always be cut about $\frac{1}{4}$-inch shorter than the total of the two holes. The ends of the dowel pins should be cut with a bevel. For the proper method of locating and drilling dowel holes, see Chapter 5.

SPLINES. A spline is a thin strip of wood or metal inserted in a groove cut in the two adjoining surfaces of a joint. It is a popular means of strengthening miter joints. The groove is cut with the radial-arm saw to a specific width and depth (page 40). A thin piece of stock is cut to fit into this groove. This stock should be cut so the grain runs at right angles to the grain of the joint.

A handy, little-known trick for clamping miter joints in cabinets is shown in the illustration. With paper sandwiched between to permit easy removal, glue a triangular block to the end of each mitered piece and let

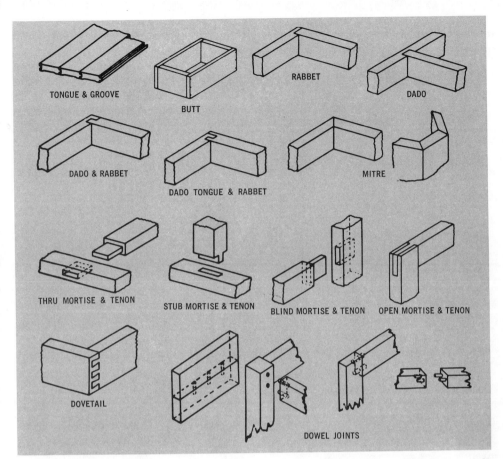

TONGUE & GROOVE

BUTT

RABBET

DADO

DADO & RABBET

DADO TONGUE & RABBET

MITRE

THRU MORTISE & TENON

STUB MORTISE & TENON

BLIND MORTISE & TENON

OPEN MORTISE & TENON

DOVETAIL

DOWEL JOINTS

WOODWORKING JOINTS. Properly constructed joints are essential for all good wood working projects. Well-constructed joints not only add to the over-all appearance of a piece of furniture, but also provide strength and durability. Sharp cutting tools and accurate measurements and cutting are necessary to produce a really tight joint. Some of the more common joints are shown here and their cuts are described in Chapters 2, 3, 4, and 5. The joints may be nailed, screwed, or glued and can be strengthened by doweling or splining.

HARDWARE INSTALLATION. The varieties of cabinet hardware are almost unlimited; so only the more common varieties used on furniture, kitchen cabinets, and similar pieces are covered here.

Full-mortise, loose-pin, and bullet-tip butt hinges are well designed for modern cabinetwork. Where two dimensions are given for butt hinges, the first indicates the length of the joint, not including the tips; the second indicates the width when the hinge is open. The size of a hinge, within certain limitations, has no relation to its weight or strength. The latter depends upon the gauge and kind of metal used.

Drop-leaf hinges are used in good furniture construction for drop leaves of tables and cabinets. The longer half of the hinge must be able to reach across the joint and have the screws set in the drop leaf. The center pin is in line with one face of the hinge, so that it may be set without gaining or cutting out for the whole hinge. However, it is necessary to gouge out a groove for the hinge joint. When these hinges are set, the center line of the pin must coincide with the center of the arc which marks the rule joint. The leaves are, of course, first cut with a drop–leaf table cutter on the shaper (see page 58).

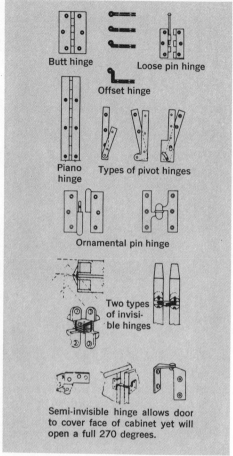

Butt hinge

Loose pin hinge

Offset hinge

Piano hinge

Types of pivot hinges

Ornamental pin hinge

Two types of invisible hinges

Semi-invisible hinge allows door to cover face of cabinet yet will open a full 270 degrees.

Although concealed hinges are not entirely hidden, only the edges of their thin joints show when the door is closed. Half of the hinge is set in the frame. Invisible hinges set in the edge of the door and frame are entirely hidden when the cabinet door is closed.

CATCHES. Probably the oldest and most common is the elbow catch, which is screwed to the back of the door. The majority of catches are of the spring variety which release by pulling the door; the elbow catch must be manually released before the door can be opened.

A newer type is the friction catch. Some of these are easily applied, being simply screwed in place, while others must be set in holes bored for them. Magnetic catches are also available.

Drawer pulls and knobs are never applied to furniture until after the finishing is complete. This makes it easier to do the finishing, since they are not in the way. There are an unlimited variety of pulls available, to fit every need and taste.

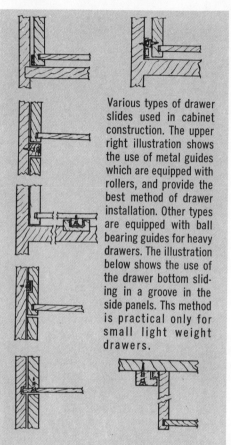

Various types of drawer slides used in cabinet construction. The upper right illustration shows the use of metal guides which are equipped with rollers, and provide the best method of drawer installation. Other types are equipped with ball bearing guides for heavy drawers. The illustration below shows the use of the drawer bottom sliding in a groove in the side panels. Ths method is practical only for small light weight drawers.

WOOD-FINISHING. The importance of a proper finish for your projects can't be overemphasized. Whether that finish is varnish, shellac, lacquer, paint, or wax, it will provide the professional appearance to make you proud of your work. If the wood grain has an attractive appearance, a natural finish may be used. The wood may be given a stain to match other pieces of furniture; or it can be bleached and given one of many attractive modern finishes. Sometimes paint may be more suitable when the wood is unattractive or when color fits into your decorative scheme. The chart on pages

179 and 180 gives the characteristics of wood and the accepted finishes.

PREPARATION OF THE WOOD. Success in finishing depends largely on the choice and preparation of the wood. The pieces should be carefully matched for grain and color, and surfaces must be clean and smooth. To obtain this smoothness, start the finishing process as the pieces are assembled. Sand each piece on the disc or drum sander as described in Chapter 8.

All marks left on the wood after construction must be removed. Rough edges left by the saw should be sanded until perfectly smooth. If they are very rough, touch them up with the jointer before sanding. Dents in wood can be eliminated by pricking the wood slightly with a sharp-pointed tool and then applying a few drops of water. The water will make the wood fibers swell back to their original shape. After the area is dry, sand the rough surface.

Joints that are not as tight as they should be can be filled with a wood filler. The seam should be cleaned and, when dry, packed with a filler such as plastic wood. Use a little more than required. An excellent home-made filler is wood glue mixed with sawdust; use the same sort of sawdust, when possible, as the wood to be filled. After the filler is dry, shave down the excess with a razor blade and sand. Cracks in end grain and other spots should also be filled.

Nailheads should be driven below the wood surface and the resulting hole filled with wood filler. Screwheads that have been countersunk can be treated in the same manner. However, a more professional method is to glue a wood plug on top of the screwhead (see page 121).

ENAMELING. Before enameling, sand the wood very smooth and be sure it is clean and dry. Apply an enamel undercoat. (In the case of fir plywood, use a sealer first and, when dry, an undercoat.) This can be either flat white paint or a special enamel. If the finish is to be a color other than white, the undercoat can be tinted either by mixing in some oil colors or by adding a little of the enamel you plan to use as the finish coat. Allow the undercoat to dry at least 24 hours and then sand the surface with fine garnet or aluminum oxide paper. Remove all traces of dust with a clean cloth dampened in turpentine.

Enamel, unlike flat paint, is flowed onto the surface. The action of the enamel removes the brush marks so the surface dries completely smooth. Once the finish has been applied, do not go back over it for additional brushing as this may leave marks which will not flow out. Be careful of accumulations of enamel around edges. These must be removed at once before they dry. In most cases, one coat of enamel will be sufficient. If it is not, allow it to dry thoroughly, give it a light sanding and dusting, and apply a second coat.

STAINING. This is usually the first operation in applying a transparent or semi-transparent finish to new wood if the natural color of the wood isn't desired. There are many types of stains, but water stains and oil stains are the most common.

Water stains may be purchased in powder form in a variety of colors and mixed as needed by dissolving in hot water. They can be sprayed or brushed. Since the water in the stain raises the grain of the wood, a previous sponging with warm water is advisable. When the wood is dry, sand it with fine paper. Then apply the stain freely and rapidly. Better penetration is obtained if the stain is used warm. Brush on the stain in long, smooth strokes, with the grain. Wiping the end grain with a cloth will prevent darkening. Other methods used to prevent darkening of end grain include (1) previous treatment with a thin glue size, (2) sponging with water immediately before staining, and (3) using a separate light stain.

Water stain will dry overnight or in 12 hours. A wash coat of 7 parts alcohol to 1 part shellac can be applied when the stain is dry. A light sanding will then remove any remaining traces of raised grain.

Manufacturers have developed stains in which water-soluble powders are dissolved in a solvent other than water. Stains of this kind are known by various trade terms, such as nongrain-raising stain, fast-to-light stain, no-sand stain, etc. They are more expensive than regular water stains because of the solvent used, but offer one of the best stains for new work. Their rapid drying makes brushing difficult, but smooth coats are easily applied by spraying. They are nonbleeding and can be used under any type of finish coat. They dry in from 10 minutes to 3 hours, depending on the type. Ready-mixed colors are numerous. Primary colors are available for mixing tints to suit individual tastes. The most commonly used oil stains are made from colors or pigments ground in linseed oil. Oil is nongrain-raising; therefore oil stains don't require previous sponging. They can be brushed or sprayed on. The main difference in technique between water and oil staining is that oil stain is dipped with a rag to remove the surplus and equalize the color. Wiping is done while the stain is wet, but time should be allowed to ensure good penetration. Immediate wiping of the end grain will eliminate darkening. Since oil stains will bleed into finishing coats of varnish and lacquer, always seal the stain with a wash coat of shellac. Avoid the use of oil stains on birch, maple, gum, cherry, or mahogany.

FILLERS AND SEALERS. A filler is used to fill the pores in coarse-grain woods before applying the final finish. A sealer is any liquid finishing material used as a first coat on close grain woods or over the filler on coarse-grain woods.

Prepared paste filler is generally the best for homecraftsmen. It may be purchased in a number of colors; select a shade slightly darker than the color of your wood, for the wood will gradually turn darker as it ages. If the desired color can't be obtained, get a light color and add colored pigment in oil.

Before using paste filler, thin it with a small amount of turpentine or naphtha until it is of the proper consistency for brushing. Wood with coarse pores will require a thicker fill than wood with small pores. About 3 pounds of filler to 1 quart of solvent is correct for mahogany, while walnut can take a slightly thinner filler (about 2½ pounds per quart of solvent).

To apply the filler, use a fairly stiff brush. Brushing is done with the grain, in order to pack the filler into the pores. In 5 to 20 minutes, the filler will start to lose its wet appearance. As soon as spots begin to get dull, take a piece of burlap and pat the filler into the pores. Clean off the surplus by wiping across the grain; finish wiping with clean rags, stroking with the grain. If the filler sets too hard for easy wiping, moisten the rag with benzine.

Inspect the entire project thoroughly. If the pores are not filled evenly, apply a second coat of slightly thinner filler immediately, wiping off in the same way. Paste filler should dry for 12 to 24 hours, unless it is a fast-drying type, which is ready in 3 to 4 hours. In any case, it is very important that the filler be bone dry before any other coating is applied. The dry filler should be sanded lightly with fine or very fine garnet or aluminum oxide paper and wiped off with a rag moistened with benzene.

Whether or not to seal the filler is largely a matter of preference. The same applies to sealing the stain coat before applying the filler, except in the case of softwoods, such as fir, which must be sealed before staining. Generally, it is good practice to seal both stain and filler. A special resin sealer is best for the job, but for many people shellac is the old standby—white shellac for light finishes and orange shellac for browns and mahoganies. The shellac is reduced with alcohol (4 to 1 for filler sealer, 7 to 1 for stain sealer), after which the shellac is poured slowly into an

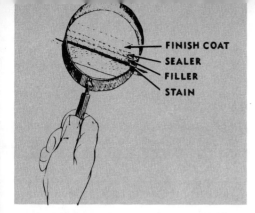

FINISH COAT
SEALER
FILLER
STAIN

equal amount or less of mixing lacquer. This mixture can be brushed on more easily than straight shellac, is almost waterproof, and dries to permit recoating in about 2 hours. Any type of sealer coat over the filler should be sanded with fine paper when dry, after which the work is ready for finishing coats of varnish or lacquer.

VARNISH FINISHES. Varnish makes an excellent transparent finish on wood, being unequaled for depth of build and possessing good durability and hardness. It brushes easily to a perfectly smooth film and dries to permit recoating in 24 to 48 hours. Varnishing should be done in a dust-free room, between 70° and 90° Fahrenheit. Some craftsmen sprinkle the floor with water to settle the dust. Before applying the varnish, dampen a piece of lintless cloth in a little varnish and wipe the surface with it. The small amount of varnish in the cloth will pick up dust which wouldn't otherwise be caught. Spread the varnish on as it comes from the can—evenly with long strokes, first with the grain, then across the grain, and then with the grain. Because varnish is slow drying, thinned shellac is often used for a sealer. The shellac dries quickly and doesn't soak into the wood, thus speeding up the drying of the varnish.

A good varnished surface usually requires three or four coats. Rub each coat down with fine steel wool or extra-fine sandpaper, after letting the varnish dry for at least 48 hours. Remove all dust from the surface, after sanding, by rubbing with a lint-free cloth moistened with turpentine or a chamois dampened with water.

Pumice and oil, followed with rottenstone and oil, will produce a finely polished surface.

Complete wood finishers, such as Deft, have recently been developed allowing the homecraftsman to complete his project in one operation. The material seals, primes, and finishes. No filler is needed, although two coats may be necessary on the more porous woods.

SHELLAC FINISHES. Shellac makes a good finish for many pieces of furniture. It is hard, quite easy to apply, dries in a few hours, and doesn't require a dustproofer. Since shellac dries very quickly, you must work fast with it, or it will become tacky and hard to handle. Never apply shellac over a damp surface, for the moisture will cause the shellac to become cloudy. Brush with the grain of the wood. Do not brush too much. For best results, dilute the shellac with alcohol. It is easier to apply thinned shellac and (unless you are experienced in applying it unthinned) you will generally get a better job. Several coats of thin shellac are best for a well-finished surface.

Standard shellac ordinarily dries in about 8 hours, although thinned shellac dries in 3 or 4 hours, ready for sanding. Go over each coat with fine sandpaper or 2/0 fine steel wool. Sandpaper with the grain of the wood. After each sanding, brush the surface and rub with a cloth dampened with benzene to remove the dust. The final rubbing or polishing should be done with an FF pumice stone and rubbing oil, using a felt pad.

LACQUER FINISHES. Roughly speaking, lacquer can be divided into two groups—brushing lacquer and spraying lacquer. Lacquers dry very rapidly. Generally, spraying lacquers dry so rapidly that they can't be applied with a brush. The solvent used with the lacquer for thinning, or as a cleaner for brushes, or a spray gun, is lacquer thinner. Thinners suitable for paint and varnish should never be used with lacquer. While paint and varnish can be applied over lacquer,

lacquer should never be applied over paint or varnish because the solvent in the lacquer will soften these base coats.

To apply brushing lacquer properly, you must work with a good deal of speed. The lacquer should be flowed on and brushed out as little as possible. Use a large brush and let it carry as much lacquer as possible without dripping. Apply the lacquer in one direction only. If a second coat is required, it must be applied with even more speed, or the solvent in the second coat will soften the first coat. By far the best way to apply lacquer is with a spray gun. This method requires special equipment—but, is the fastest and easiest way to a good lacquer finish.

RUBBING WITH PUMICE AND ROTTEN-STONE. A fine finish for varnish, lacquer, and shellac is obtained by rubbing with pumice or rottenstone. Mix the pumice with either water or oil (paraffin or mineral), and use a felt pad to rub the paste over the finished surface. Rub with the grain. Use pumice with oil, not with water, on a shellac finish. Rub until the desired finish is obtained. Rottenstone is much finer than pumice and is used in the same manner, usually following a rubbing with pumice. If water is used with either pumice or rottenstone, it makes the mixture cut faster and produces a duller finish. When rubbing edges, corners, and high spots, be careful not to cut through finish. Clean the surface thoroughly with a soft rag after rubbing.

WAX FINISHES. A wax finish has a pleasing eggshell gloss and is satisfactory for furniture as well as for floors and woodwork. Fill the wood and give it a sealing coat of thinned shellac, lacquer, or varnish, and allow to dry. Sandpaper lightly before applying the wax. Rub the wax on the surface, a little at a time, with a soft cloth. Allow to dry for about 20 minutes, then rub hard with a soft cloth. Several coats are usually required.

BLEACHING OR "BLONDING." Bleach-ing lightens the color of wood by means of chemicals. Apart from the bleaching process, the so-called blond finishes do not differ in any way from other finishes. Not all blond finishes are secured by bleaching. Maple, birch, and other light-colored woods are successfully blonded by the use of a pigmented undercoat. This subject is treated at the end of this chapter.

There are several prepared commercial bleaches which are high-powered enough to give nearly white tones on walnut and mahogany in a single application. The procedure for applying these bleaches varies with the brand, and the manufacturer's directions must be followed. After the work is completely dry, it should be sanded lightly with very fine sandpaper to remove any chemical residue and to clean up wood fibers lifted by the bleaching solution.

Wood is usually bleached a bit more than is required for the final finish. The color is brought back to the desired shade with a light application of non-grain-raising stain, applied in such a manner as to equalize any variations in color. The stain is followed by a wash coat of shellac or lacquer, after which the regular schedule of filler and top coat completes the finish.

BLOND SEALERS. Excellent blond finishes can be obtained without bleaching by using a surface color or blond sealer. This is a very satisfactory method of treating naturally light woods. Add white lacquer enamel to clear lacquer, or, if an amber effect is desired, add tan to clear lacquer. Blond sealers of this kind can be purchased ready mixed. A uniform, light coat of the sealer will produce a satisfactory blond color without obscuring the natural grain of the wood. This blonding technique is perfect on maple and birch and can be used on walnut and mahogany to produce a pleasing tone, a little lighter than the natural color of the wood. When overdone on dark-colored woods, it gives the wood a painted appearance and the effect isn't pleasing.

CHAPTER 11

WORKING WITH THE NEW BUILDING MATERIALS

The radial-arm machine's versatility has been proven in the previous chapters of this book. But, its versatility doesn't end with wood; it can be used to perform many cutting tasks on the so-called new building materials such as plastics, asbestos-cement board, plasterboard, insulation board, marble, honeycomb panels, aluminum, etc.

Some of these materials may be cut with the standard woodworking blades. However, for most cutting operations on harder surface materials special blades such as the non-ferrous and ferrous saw blades, carbide tipped saw blades, etc. (see page 130), and abrasive cut-off wheels must be employed. The abrasive wheels are thin discs, the size of a saw blade, which look like cardboard. They're made of such materials as glass-fiber cloth impregnated with resins and hard abrasives. Mounted on the radial-arm machine, they'll cut and grind materials you never dreamed of working so easily—heavy metals, pipe, stone, concrete—jobs that would be difficult and time consuming with a hacksaw or chisel—or wouldn't be possible at all.

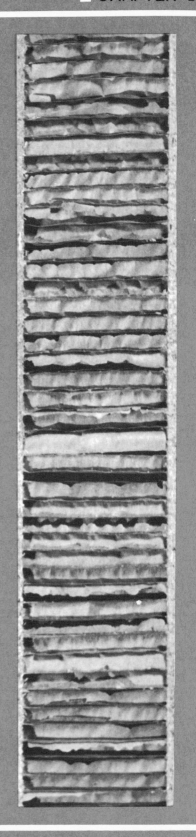

Unlike saw blades, there are only two basic types of abrasive cut-off wheels. One is aluminum oxide, which is used on metals, especially the hard ones like iron, steel, hard brass and hard bronze. The other is silicon carbide for use on nonmetallic materials, such as stone, concrete, ceramics, brick tile, plastics, asbestos-cement boards, plasterboard, carbon, brake linings and insulation boards. This type will also do a good job on the softer metals such as aluminum, and is sometimes recommended for cutting small-diameter steel rods.

Although these wheels possess remarkable strength, they'll chip or break if improperly handled. The feed should be steady and even at all times and of sufficient pressure to pre-vent glazing of the wheel. Remember that an abrasive wheel cuts on its side as well as its edge. Try to keep the work as straight as possible or the discs may snow-plow, cutting a wide and sloppy groove. However, the work shouldn't be forced too much, since this will shorten the life of the wheel considerably. Because cutoff wheels are mounted on the motor arbor in the same manner as a saw blade, the safety guard should be used. Once mounted, you can make the same basic cuts with the cutoff wheels as those made with a saw blade in wood.

Now let's take a look at some new building materials and how they can be worked.

PLYWOOD. While plywood is a wood product and has been shown in several of the illustrations in Chapters 2—8, it has several working characteristics that should be fully discussed. Although it has been manufactured for some time, plywood did not become popular with home craftsmen until after World War II. Today, it is one of the most popular materials used.

When cutting plywood on a radial-arm machine the good face of the material should be up. The best saw blade to use is the special fine-tooth plywood type (see page 15). This blade has a thin-rim taper, ground for clearance, and has little or no tooth set. It therefore makes cuts with a satin smooth finish ideal for glue joints. The radial-arm saw can rip 4-foot-wide panels right down the middle with ease. It's easier to handle large panels alone if you build an extension support with a roller; such a support can have a base of its own or it can be clamped to a saw horse. For sawing curves, use a 15- or 20-tooth blade in the saber saw.

The plywood operations of the various other attachments for the radial-arm machine—the dado head, shaper, router, boring bits, etc.—are handled in the same manner as regular wood. For ¾-inch plywood, the dowel and spline joint is the most commonly used in joining panels. The spline, usually about ¼ inch thick and ⅝ inch wide, is continuous and may be made from plywood. The dowels (usually No. 7 or 8 spiral) are on centers anywhere from 4 to 10 inches. The tongue-and-groove joint is a standard treatment. The tongue is usually ¼ inch wide and approximately $5/_{16}$ inch deep. When bowing panels into place, the sides of the tongue are chamfered slightly. The groove is always made a little larger than the tongue. Dowels are also used to provide extra joint security. For thinner plywood, joint treatments recommended for wall paneling can be used. Reinforcement strips must be used behind the thinner materials (it is a good idea for thicker material, too). Glue should be used on all panel joints.

Corner butt joints are the easiest to make and are suitable for ¾-inch plywood. For thinner panels, use a reinforcing block or nailing strip to make a stronger joint. In all cases, glue will make the joint many times stronger than nails or screws alone. Frame construction makes it possible to reduce weight by using thinner plywood.

When making miters of plywood, there is sometimes a swelling of the wood, causing the joint to open, especially when water-base glues are employed. To avoid this, cut the miter so it is left slightly open at the back. Although this necessitates a corner strip to reinforce the joint, the little extra work pays off in a perfect fit and a good-looking corner. The hardwood corner is another possibility. Any of the standard corner joints can be used. This method depends on the availability of matching hardwood. It is advisable to keep the dimension of the piece so that stock wood sizes can be used, such as ⅞ or 1⅛ inches.

Plywood edges can be a problem. If care is not exercised, the finished job will be bonded with raw edges that resemble half-healed scars. First, check the design of the piece to be built. Even with plain butt joints, there are an astonishing number of ways to assemble a simple box, and each one makes a difference in the number or position of visible edges. By using rabbets and miters, a little thought at the design stage can reduce the problem. Consider where the piece of furniture will be located, what surface will be exposed, and what finish you will use.

Possibly the best treatment for edge grain is shown here in detail A. Two 45° cuts are made from the underside, completely through the wood, the small piece is removed, and the end is bent as shown. By this method a continuous grain is shown—even on the ends.

A solid piece of material—that is, solid hardwood—in the shape of a T in cross section can be glued to the piece of plywood so that, when the edge is viewed, it will appear as solid lumber (detail B). The procedure shown in detail C is the same, except that the piece of lumber is triangular in cross section. Cutting the edge at an angle, as shown in detail D, is a neat and cheap method; the edge grain may be painted or stained to match the panel.

It is also possible to bead the edge

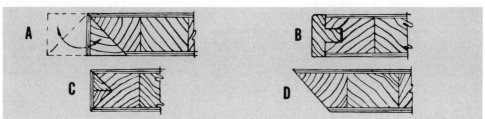

or to glue a beading strip or molding to the edge. A mitered framing strip, secured by glue and by brads that have been set and puttied, is a very effective treatment, especially for table and desk tops. Molding made with the shaper attachment is also good for the exposed top edges of a desk. Do not overlook common half- or quarter-round molding; its width may be greater than the edge width. Aluminum veneer cap molding may also be used, or thin veneer can be glued to the edge grain.

A new veneer tape, available in several wood grains, can be obtained. It consists of a precut ¾-inch strip of thin wood veneer with its own adhesive on the back. After the tape is applied according to manufacturer's instructions, it is finished exactly the same as the panel faces—with stain, varnish, lacquer, or paint. The effect is that of an expensive solid panel.

PLASTIC-COATED PLYWOOD. Plastic-surfaced plywoods combine many of the desirable characteristics of a phenolic-plastic laminate with those of plywood. For machining, much the same techniques can be used as for unsurfaced plywood. However, it is desirable to use certain variations to protect the smooth plastic surfacing. These are general suggestions for all types of plastic-surfaced plywood. In using these panels, you should also follow the manufacturer's instruc-

tions for the specific product involved.

Handle plastic-coated plywoods so that the saw cut won't chip the plastic overlay. While either the standard combination plywood or rip blades may be employed, it saves sharpening time to use carbide-tipped ones if you plan to do much sawing. The 20-tooth blade should be used when saber sawing.

Plastic-surface plywoods may be bonded to each other or to wood by cold gluing with resorcinol-formaldehyde, phenolformaldehyde, or urea-formaldehyde adhesives. The manufacturer's instructions should be followed and the joint should be placed under the highest pressure attainable. Most adhesives of these types require aging for several days before they reach full strength. When you glue plastic to plastic, use a minimum of adhesive; a somewhat heavier spread when gluing plastic surfaces to wood. If a plastic finish is highly glazed, sanding lightly with fine sandpaper before the adhesive is applied will give maximum bonding strength.

Use as small a casing nail as possible to nail plastic-coated plywood. If you use a large nail, the plastic may crack next to the nail hole. Nails should be driven carefully to avoid marring the plastic surface when appearance or water-shedding properties are important. Place nails at least ¼ inch from the edge of the panel to avoid cracking the surface.

LAMINATED-PLASTIC MATERIAL. Decorative laminated-plastic materials are available in sheet form or already glued to ¾-inch plywood. If the material is in sheet form, you must apply it yourself to a plywood base. Recently developed adhesives make this application possible without clamps, presses, or other pressure devices. While you should follow the manufacturer's instructions to the letter, the following four basic steps will help you do a perfect bonding job with contact or pressure-sensitive adhesives:

■ Be sure the surfaces are clean prior to being covered with a glossy film of adhesive. (When the adhesive is dry, the entire surface should look glossy. Dull spots mean that another coat of adhesive is necessary.)

■ Apply cement to both surfaces and allow it to dry. (Test dryness by pressing a small piece of heavy kraft paper onto the cemented surface. If no cement sticks to the paper, it is dry.)

■ The temperature of both cemented surfaces must be 70° Fahrenheit or above at the time of bonding.

■ Apply the sheet in its proper location; roll the surface thoroughly, using heavy pressure on a hand roller. (Make certain every part of the two surfaces are brought into contact.)

No sustained pressure is required to create a permanent bond.

The plywood used for tables and cabinet tops is usually ¾ inch thick, whether of interior or exterior grade. The exterior type should definitely be used for sink and vanity counter tops. Interior or non-waterproof types may be acceptable for furniture shelves, coffee-table tops, etc.

Although laminated plastics are harder than marble, they are surprisingly easy to cut. As a general rule carbide-tipped blades are the most durable, but they must be handled carefully because they tend to be brittle. The thin-rim combination or plywood blades are very good (they make the best cut), but they dull rather quickly when cutting this material. Either a 10- or 15-tooth blade may be used with the saber saw. The router bit may also be used to cut laminated plastics and is considered ideal for making sink cutouts, etc. When making any cuts, regardless of the tool, be sure the decorative face is up.

Exposed edges of laminated plastic should always be given a slight bevel, as a sharp edge is dangerous and susceptible to chipping. Beveling also corrects any unevenness resulting from the sawing operation. Use either a fine-toothed flat file or a fine-set plane, and cut down from the decorative side.

HARDBOARD. Properties and characteristics of hardboard panels make them suitable for interior and exterior use in new construction or remodeling of residential, farm, commercial and industrial buildings. Since hardboards are made of wood, with no artificial fillers or binders, they may be easily worked and applied by the usual carpentry methods. A wide variety of surface treatments is easy to produce. Simple bends and curves are easily formed. Finishing presents no special problems—paint, enamel, lacquer, stain, shellac and varnish may be applied by ordinary methods.

Fundamentally, there are two types of hardboards—standard and tempered. Both are available in various thicknesses and textures. However, as with any good product, the wrong usage can result in unsatisfactory results. Standard types do not have as high a water-resistant or wearing quality as tempered boards. They are more adaptable for interior walls, cabinets and places where moisture or abrasion are no problem. The wearing and water resistant qualities of the tempered variety make them an excellent flooring and siding material. They are satisfactory for exterior applications or wherever high or changing humidity may prevail as in bathrooms and basements.

Perforated hardboard or peg-board offers a completely new idea in wall surfacing. Both useful and decorative items may be arranged and rearranged on either smooth or embossed panels without in any way defacing the wall. There are over 60 metal hangers available which are instantly interchangeable and self-locking without the use of any tools and make perforated hardboard panels adaptable to an infinite variety of applications.

As has already been stated, hardboard can be cut with standard combination or plywood blades, but when extensive cutting is to be done, use a carbide-tipped blade, especially when using tempered hardboard. The 10- or 15-tooth blade should be employed when saber sawing.

WALL BOARD. The range of material classed as wall board is wide. They include such products as asbestos-cement board, gypsum or plaster-board, fiberboard and insulation board. They are all available in panel form and some come in predecorated finishes.

As a rule, you can cut asbestos-cement board, gypsum board, or plaster-board by first scoring the material, then snapping it off. But, you can get accurate cuts on these materials by placing a silicon-carbide cutoff wheel on your radial-arm machine.

Fiberboard and insulation boards are easy to cut with the standard combination blade, but the most accurate results can be obtained by em-

ploying a hollow-ground or a plywood type. Most types of acoustical ceiling tiles are cut in the same manner. When using a saber saw, the 20-tooth blade will do a good job.

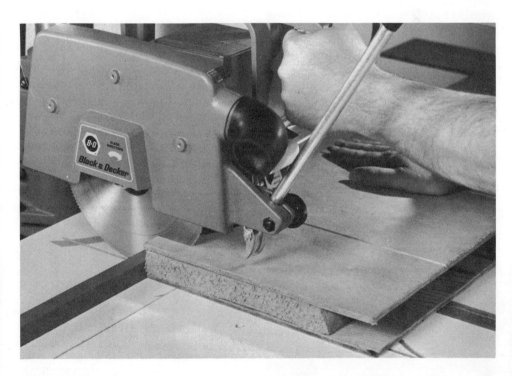

HONEYCOMB PANELS. All the possibilities of this new building material have yet to be fully explored by either the building trade or the home craftsman. This material may take the place of the standard wood-stud type of construction now in use in most of our homes. While there are several types of core designs employed, basically these units are two finished-panel

surfaces separated by a laminated honeycomb core. They are available in two general styles—for load-bearing walls and non-load-bearing partitions.

While exact cutting instructions vary with each manufacturer of honeycomb panels (be sure to follow the manufacturer's directions to the letter), the carbide-tipped cutoff and plywood blades will do a good job.

ASPHALT, VINYL AND RUBBER FLOOR TILE. Fitting corners around fixtures, holes for plumbing, and cutting irregular pieces are frequent problems encountered in laying floor tiles of all kinds. The saber saw attachment of the radial-arm machine handles such tedious work with ease and neatness. The 7- or 10-tooth blades may be used to cut these materials. Although these materials can be scored and cut along straight edges with ordinary tools (or you can cut them quickly with a silicon-carbide cutoff wheel), it is often difficult to get neatly cut curved sections that will fit accurately. Use a piece of cardboard to get the correct shape and size of the piece and then follow the pattern directly on the workpiece. Asphalt, rubber tile and even some of the new plastic materials may be cut in this manner.

One precaution must be taken when handling the asphalt type of floor tile. Be sure the room temperature is above 65° and that the tiles are warmed to room temperature. When they are cold, they are very brittle and will snap easily even when being handled for flat, open-floor installation. The other types of material present no such problem.

CERAMIC TILE. If you have ever attempted to get a straight break line on a ceramic tile after having scored it with a glass cutter, you know what a blessing it is to be able to cut the tiles on a radial-arm machine equipped with a silicon-carbide cutoff wheel. As with marble, take shallow cuts, say about 1/8 inch deep on each pass. Curved shapes or smoothed edges may be obtained by using the side of the wheel. Cut the tile with the glazed surface on the table top.

FIBERGLAS PLASTIC MATERIAL. Fiberglas-reinforced plastic paneling makes a good roof for a patio, shower-door for your bathtub, screen for room divider, flower box and planter, and many other things around the home. They come in many attractive colors and designs in flat or corrugated sheet forms. It's easy to "do-it-yourself" with this material since plastic cuts well with a radial saw and is simple to nail to framing. It requires only light framing because of its own rigidity. The panels can be cut to size with a silicon-carbide wheel or a metal cutting blade.

FLAGSTONE, BRICK AND OTHER MASONRY UNITS. Flagstone and brick can be cut by making several passes through the material with a silicon-carbide cutoff wheel, lowering the blade approximately 1/8 inch, until you're through. For rough cuts, you can score the stone or brick and then break it clean with a mason's hammer or a brick chisel. Since most masonry units — either cinder or concrete blocks—are too thick for passing the wheel through from one side, it must be turned over and cut from the other side or it can be scored on all four sides so it will break cleanly.

ALUMINUM AND LIGHT METAL. Light metal, especially aluminum, is becoming more and more a home shop material. While all aluminums can be cut with either an aluminum oxide, silicon-carbide cutoff wheel, or a non-ferrous metal cutting blade, one type —aptly called do-it-yourself aluminum—can be cut with any standard radial-arm saw blade. Always remember to advance the saw into the metal slowly and evenly. While it is entirely practical to make long, heavy cuts in aluminum, as when ripping bar or angle sections, it is important to avoid continuous cutting with a heavy feed. This heats up the saw-blade tips and causes them to pick up aluminum particles which partially weld themselves to the blade. To prevent such metal pickup, stop the feed occasionally and allow the blade to run unloaded for a short time to keep it cool. Also, while the blade is at rest, lubricate it with a paraffin block or old candle to reduce friction. Check the set of your saw if it tends to bind after lubricating. If the saw drags when making a heavy cut, stop it and inspect the blade. Remove any aluminum particles sticking to the teeth by flipping them off with a knife or screwdriver. A wire brush is also excellent for cleaning saw teeth. Then, reduce your rate of feed to avoid "leading up" the teeth again.

To cut thin-wall tubing, it's wise to hold it in a V-block. The block can be clamped to the guide fence and tubing permitted to project beyond the block, or the block may have a saw kerf to permit the passage of the blade.

As previously stated, aluminum oxide cutoff wheels should be used on metals, especially the hard ones that take shallow cuts. Allow the work to cool between cuts. When cutting metal—anytime you use the abrasive wheel—wear goggles to protect your eyes from flying sparks or particles.

In general, light metal can be cut on the saber saw with the same techniques as wood. Use either a 15- or 20-tooth blade. Thin sheet metal should be shellacked to a wood base to prevent burring on the underside. Take it easy when cutting these materials. Never force them against the blade or cut them when they start to heat up.

MARBLE. In the last few years marble has made a comeback in our modern homes. It is employed in furniture which can be used for serving hot meals and in outdoor furniture which will withstand the weather.

While a few soft marbles can be cut with either carbide-tipped or non-ferrous saw blades, the majority will require a cutoff wheel. It is usually better to make a number of very shallow cuts instead of one big one, to avoid straining the blade. You can also use the side of an abrasive wheel like a sanding disc to smooth the edges after cutting and to shape curves. When sawing, wear goggles to protect the eyes from flying particles.

PLASTICS. Clear, glass-like acrylic plastics can also be cut on the radial saw using either a non-ferrous saw blade or the silicon-carbide abrasive wheel. Keep the protective paper on the plastic until you're ready to buff. The buffing operation is done in the same way as for glass. These plastics can also be cut with a 15- or 20-tooth saber saw blade.

CHAPTER 12

GETTING THE MOST FROM THE RADIAL-ARM MACHINE

The radial-arm machine is an important investment. The previous chapters have told you what it will do and how to do it. Now, in this chapter we would like to explain how you can put these methods to use in your own home. In so doing, you will save many times your original investment and have fun at the same time.

Six areas of home improvement are mentioned in this chapter. When you do-it-yourself, savings easily average 40 to 50 percent and, in some cases, run as high as 60 to 70 percent of the usual cost. Do any *one* of the suggested projects yourself, and the saving realized will, more than likely, be more than the original cost of your radial-arm machine. It also guarantees maximum savings by utilizing the lowest cost, but entirely serviceable, materials; accomplishment of many jobs which simply can't be done by hand; and completion of the project in a fraction of the time required by hand methods alone, or even by the use of several other power tools.

It has been stated many times in this book that the radial-arm machine is versatile. When you are doing a major project such as those suggested

here, another facet of its versatility is that it can be easily carried by two men from its home in the shop to the site of the project, if desired. (If mounted on the leg stand, it can easily be rolled to any location.) Once at the project site, it is ready to help you obtain the professional results you want for the finished job.

Let's see how you can get the most out of your radial-arm machine by discussing some specific home-improvement projects.

GETTING THE MOST FROM YOUR BASEMENT. Living space in most homes is much too valuable to let the basement remain a gloomy dungeon. Here your skill and imagination have free play, for almost anything can be built into a basement. You may wish to devote most of the space to an adult recreation or rumpus room, a home gymnasium for the youngsters, or a home–shop built around your radial-arm machine. But at the same time you can provide for a gardner's corner, a built-in playpen with a raised floor, and a great deal of general storage space.

When you plan a basement room, first consider its use. Try to visualize the best materials for carrying out the plan. Survey the space giving consideration to utility and the least interference with other family activities.

Check the following thoroughly: Encroachment on needed laundry space; location of heat ducts, pipes and other overhead obstructions; floor conditions; location of windows; wall treatment necessary for finished appearance; head room; utilization of under-stairs space; location of floor drains, clean-outs, etc.

Plot the location of new walls if the room is to be closed off from the rest of the basement. Locate built-in serving counter or bar as far from the entrance as possible, insuring the greatest comfort with the least confusion. For the wall materials themselves, you have a wide choice: plasterboard in plain or wood-grain

effects, wall board and hardboard in sheets, tile, plank, real wood planks such as knotty pine or pecky cypress, slab wood for log-cabin effects, and plywood. If real wood or plywood is employed, it's advisable to back-prime it with a resin sealer or a good paint primer before erection.

For the ceiling, insulating and acoustical tiles are the most popular. These materials, available in various decorative effects, not only stop the transmission of sound to the upstair rooms, but will prevent dust and drafts from infiltrating the upper floors. For the floors, asphalt tiles will provide a lasting surface that is both colorful and waterproof.

The basement shown in the photograph has many unique features. For instance, the accordion doors are made from 3/4-inch plywood, cut to the correct size. After each door is hung on four concealed hinges and finished, ordinary playing cards are mounted in the center of a 7-inch painted band (ordinary household cement will do the job), and varnished.

The concealed bookcase-cabinet on the far wall has a backing of 1/4-inch and shelves of 3/4-inch fir plywood. The edges of the shelves are banded with strips of hardwood molding which can be made easily on the radial-arm machine (shaper attachment).

The big, comfortable bench-and-back combination is easy to make. The bench rests on a 2– by 4-inch rail secured through the wall material, into the masonry. The triangular braces on the underside are spaced to fit against furring strips on the wall. The back can be hung on the wall with large, slotted keyhole hangers on each furring strip. The back and seat are each made of one piece of foam rubber and covered with plastic or cloth with the edges turned over and tacked. The back is secured to the board and built out to a comfortable slant.

Here are four other possible basement layouts that may help you in your planning.

AN ATTIC CAN LEAD A USEFUL LIFE.

Adding rooms is a wise way to utilize empty attic space. The space and basic framing are there and you have a wide choice of room and storage arrangements. The room layout in each attic, of course, presents a different problem, depending on usable area and the roof's pitch. In general, if the rise of the roof is less than 8 feet, there will not be sufficient headroom for a usable room. The minimum headroom is considered to be 6 feet, 6 inches, and the average person requires 4 feet of headroom when seated. Therefore, the points at which walls 4 feet high will intersect the sloping rafters determine the width of the prospective room. Unless the house is unusually large, a rise less than one-third of the span leaves attic space with too little headroom. The length of the room will be dependent upon the length of the house, the placement of the stairs, the location of interior chimneys or any other obstruction.

Don't be discouraged if your headroom doesn't seem enough. A pair of dormers are easily built and will greatly increase the usable floor area in the attic. Also, sometimes it pays to "raise the roof" and it's not as difficult as you might think. The roof is jacked up, side walls are extended upward, and "presto"—you have a taller house with the space you need upstairs. This idea is especially useful where lot lines and landscape restrictions prevent expansion on any side. It is also less expensive than adding an extension to the first floor of your house.

If the attic is small, or only one room is to be finished off, the problem is relatively easy; the plan generally depends upon the location of the stairway. Where space exists for two or more rooms, preliminary measurements of the available area should be made into a rough floor plan so you can visualize just how the location of the stairway will influence the arrangement of the rooms. In most small houses, the attic stairs are centrally located, providing an ideal layout with rooms opening from a small central hall. Where the stairway enters the attic at one end, however, there is seldom sufficient headroom available for a lateral hallway, and the floor plan must permit entry into a living or general-purpose room first, with the bedroom at the opposite end. Generally it is best to keep the number of rooms in the attic to a minimum in order to avoid very small rooms.

Another point to keep in mind when planning the attic is to allow maximum storage space, both in the rooms and under the eaves, for all the equipment you would normally store in an unfinished attic.

If an attic is to be made livable, it must be as well ventilated and lighted as any other rooms in the house. Many attics have only one or two windows, often fixed. If this is the case, additional windows may be

added in the side walls, or dormers can be built.

Well-placed dormers relieve a monotonous roof line, too, and can actually improve the exterior appearance of your home. Unless the house is so located that one side of the sloping roof faces to the rear, two dormers are usually needed to balance each other in appearance. For widths over 8 feet the shed or Dutch type of dormer should be used. Shed dormers, because of their greater width, offer a maximum of headroom and light.

If you are not familiar with the type of carpentry required to frame a dormer, it is a good idea to have this part of the job done by professional help. As soon as the dormers are in place, you can take over and finish the job without difficulty thanks to the helping hand given you by the radial-arm machine.

It is possible to get sufficient light without the use of dormers. As shown here, the end walls of the room were opened up to provide big handsome windows fitted under the roof slope. Existing studs in the wall and ceiling surfaces were paneled with fir plywood finished with a tinted clear varnish that softened the grain contrast in the wood. Rather than let the hard-to-use area under the lower part of the roof slope go to waste, the space was utilized by building desks and drawers right into the walls. Writing surfaces slide out of the way when not in use. Two of the study areas built into the walls also serve admirably as drawer and storage space, particularly for students. The wall above the stairwell has doors which provide access to the space behind the walls. There is another entry from the stairs to the same area. The floors are asphalt tile laid over a plywood base which provides a smooth, solid, inexpensive foundation for any kind of resilient flooring.

ADDITIONAL ATTIC IMPROVEMENT IDEAS

Alcove under the eaves forms a cozy sleeping nook. When not in use, the doors close to blend with the wall paneling.

Built-in beds and drawers lined up along one wall add to the spacious feeling by making good use of the low headroom space.

The *under eaves storage unit* makes good use of the awkward area under the sloping attic ceiling.

A NEW WING ADDS VALUE AND LIVABILITY. If you don't have an attic which can be finished, you can often solve that "more room for a growing family" problem by adding a new room or wing. This increase of your family's living space may take the form of enclosing a porch, making an all-weather family room out of a breezeway, raising the roof over an

Vanity-desk built-in dormer area makes good use of ordinarily wasted space.

airing deck and gaining a room, converting an attached garage into a bedroom, or planning an actual extension.

First, decide what your needs are. Perhaps a living room, a dining area, or another bedroom would help to reduce the lack of living space. Having decided what addition is needed, next check municipal zoning and building codes and the restrictive clauses in your deed. Know how much of the lot your house can cover and how close you can build to the lot line. There may be limitations on materials, building heights, and roof slopes. For instance, an enclosed porch that becomes part of the house is often subject to more rigid building regulations.

In most modern homes the attached garage offers the best room for space improvement. Converting it into a bright new playroom is generally a quick and simple job because it involves no major structural changes. The car? An inexpensive carport will do nicely in most climates.

An *enclosed breezeway* was built to connect this unattached garage to the house.

The *garage door* opening offers an already framed area for a large picture window. The garage roof was extended to the left to form the carport.

This *roomy double garage* was transformed into a new family room. New carport was added at the other end of the house.

BRINGING THE KITCHEN UP-TO-DATE.

Possibly the easiest way to justify your purchase of a radial-arm machine to your wife is to suggest bringing her kitchen up-to-date with modern cabinets and built-ins since, from a woman's point of view, no room is more important.

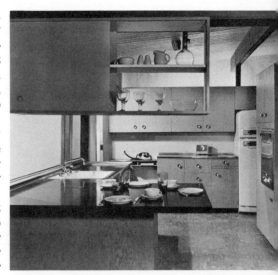

Intensive research has been done by home economists and engineers on the best labor-saving arrangements for kitchens as well as new and better equipment to carry them out.

Leading home planners agree that the kitchen should be divided into three primary work centers—one for food storage and preparation, one for cooking and serving, and one for cleaning. These three functional centers, each with fixed equipment, plumbing fixtures, base and wall cabinets, counter surfaces, portable appliances, utensils and dishes, all in the proper relationship to each other, make up the normal kitchen. The organization of each center is as important as its relationship to the others.

The food storage and preparation center is planned around the refrigerator where perishable food is kept, the storage cabinets for some staple supplies and utensils, and the counter surfaces where the food is prepared for cooking. Proper arrangement here should make it possible to prepare either a single recipe or food for an entire meal with a minimum number of steps. There should be ample counter surface next to the refrigerator for food preparation. Since food preparation often requires the use of the sink, the ideal arrangement is a continuous counter from refrigerator to sink. You should allow enough space between the counter and the underside of the wall cabinets for the mixer (16 inches is considered a minimum).

The cooking and serving center is planned around the range, with shelves or cupboards for cooking utensils and serving dishes so food can be served as hot as possible. For convenience in serving, this area should be near the eating center in the kitchen or near the door to the dining room. A clearance of 30 inches should be allowed between the range top and the underside of the wall cabinet.

The cleaning center is planned around the sink, with a stack counter, a refuse receptacle, and the drainboard adjoining. The cabinets for dishes should be within easy reach. Since water is used for both food preparation and cooking, this center should always be located between the preparation center and the cooking center. Both sides of the sink should have generous counter space, so necessary for cleaning-up. Wherever possible, sinks should be equipped with

double drainboards. A splashboard from 3 to 8 inches high should be behind the sink itself. Lower ones, from 1 to 3 inches, at the back of all counters make cleaning easier.

Research has shown that approximately 6 square feet of wall-cabinet storage space (shelf area) must be allowed for each occupant of the home, plus 12 square feet for entertaining and accumulation. Thus the wall-cabinet storage is calculated: 6 square feet of shelf area times three persons equals 18; 18 plus 12 square feet equals 30 square feet. Base cabinets should occupy all the space not required by the range, refrigerator, and sink.

Actually, the first step in planning any alteration of an existing kitchen is a thorough study of the routine of kitchen work in relation to the fixed equipment in the room. The sink, doors, and windows, for example, are generally considered fixed items which would be expensive or impossible to move. A motion study might disclose a way of using fixed pieces in their present locations and adding cupboards or counters for extra working and storage space. Your local public library carries a number of books that will yield valuable hints on methods of studying motions made in routine kitchen work.

After you have made a motion study of movements in the preparation of meals, draw a plan of the kitchen to scale in order to study the most advantageous rearrangement of the equipment. Locate all fixed equipment on the plan. A circle drawn around the door will indicate the space taken up by its swing.

Next make paper patterns, to scale, of such movable equipment as refrigerator, range, and tables; cut them out and move them about on the plan to find the best locations for each item. An exchange of ideas among the members of the household may bring out workable suggestions for placing equipment that will help in establishing the final arrangement. Always remember that paper plans are easily changed while permanent equipment, once made and installed, will remain in place even if it does not serve its purpose. Forethought will save needless expense. A long-range plan makes it possible to install small units one at a time—a convenience that a home craftsman can appreciate. The photographs in this section show several kitchen improvements that will make any wife happy that her husband purchased a radial-arm machine.

BUILT-INS FOR YOUR HOME. By built-in units we simply mean furniture units that appear to be attached to the structural parts of the house. The most important function of built-in furniture is saving space. This has become increasingly important as homes have become smaller, with rooms reduced both in number and size. In many cases building-in provides additional storage, drawer, and closet space simply by using waste space to the best advantage. With proper planning, they offer greater convenience and grace to a room by eliminating several pieces and replacing them with one well-planned unit. In addition, it gives any room a personal, custom-built look, which ready-made movable pieces can't achieve.

The conveniences that built-in units give the homemaker are invaluable. It makes cleaning easier because it is built or fitted flush to the floor and wall, and therefore allows no space for dust and dirt to accumulate.

Apart from making the most of small rooms, built-in units are useful in dividing large ones. Sometimes a more livable scheme can be worked out by building units to act as a room divider, which is cheaper and often more satisfactory than building a partition or wall. Also in older houses

wonderful things can be done by camouflaging undesirable architectural elements with built-ins. By careful planning of built-in furniture you may get extra seating area, desk, or work space, and at the same time improve your home.

Built-in sofa is fine for any room corner. The cabinet under the 12-inch stair recess houses the record player at the right, and forms the back for the built-in seats.

Wall storage unit includes desk, built-in bar, shelves, cabinets to replace space-wasteful conventional furnishings.

This *entertainment wall and room divider* does a wonderful job of combining the answer to many storage problems with a useful and ingenious room partition. To begin with, the room divider functions beautifully in your main room, creating a dining room out of part of your living room, if needed, and adding privacy to both. Or it can create an eye-pleasing vestibule in homes with front doors opening into the living room. Either end of this unit may be placed against the wall. Or you may want to build the unit for use along one wall in living room, den, or recreation area. It's a true storage center including three

A *free standing entry closet* shields living area from a doorway. Both sides of unit have storage closets, drawers.

roomy cabinets, each with colorful sliding doors (the bottom picture on our back cover shows the room divider in its actual colors), a four-drawer chest, three shelves for books or knick-knacks, and a roomy liquor cabinet with an access door on each side of the divider. It provides room for your high-fidelity phonograph and speakers. One section will hold the turntable and well removed from it, up at the top, is an insulated sound chamber for two speakers. It does so much for every member of the family, and combines all its uses into one attractive unit making it almost irresistible.

An excellent *desk-built-in storage unit* and *hi-fi-radio unit* arrangement is fine for any den or family room. The storage unit features sliding doors.

Built-in bunks are ideal for growing boys—they're as neat and trim as a clipper ship.

IDEAS FOR OUTDOOR LIVING.

Everyone likes to eat outdoors when the hot summer months descend upon us. The cool breezes and fresh air stimulate the appetite and make every meal a feast. But, appetites are often lost when we consider the trouble of serving a meal outdoors. As shown here, this add-on shed was designed to be the perfect solution—it does away with all the bothersome fetch-and-carry work and makes outdoor dining just as easy and convenient as dining indoors. The shed has a spacious, well-planned barbecue cupboard that holds pots, pans and utensils, as well as a table that folds down to provide table space for four or more people. In addition, there are two peg-board-lined walk-in closets that can solve all of your outdoor storage problems. The smaller closet has enough space to accommodate all of your garden tools and equipment, including the lawnmower. The larger closet is just right for storing extra tables and chairs, and any other items that may need protection from the weather.

Another popular exterior structure is the store-all garden pergola shown here. Equally adaptable to a formal garden setting, spacious grounds or even a small backyard, this handsome structure is geared to the practicalities of life in the suburbs. It's designed to be a center of attraction as well as a center of activity. The storage space is more than ample for gardening tools, outdoor barbecue equipment and other items, and the attractive slatted benches at the base of the unit are perfect for displaying colorful potted plants. A few seat cushions placed on these benches will quickly turn the structure into a barbecue shed. Although the building materials —plywood and framing lumber— have been used with a free hand to achieve an interesting, oriental design, it is remarkably inexpensive to build. The roof of this unit is an adaptation of a low-cost system originally worked out for farm structures. The plywood on the roof is lapped like giant shingles and left uncovered. The two front storage spaces underneath the roof are four feet wide and two feet deep. The rear two storage spaces are shallower, just one foot deep, so that you can reach smaller items easily. On the backs of all the doors there is a shelf arrangement which stiffens the panels and provides extra storage space.

The range of outdoor living projects that can be undertaken and com-

pleted with the help of your radial-arm machine is wide. From the playhouse for children (left) to the outdoor living room (right), there are countless woodworking projects available to the handyman.

MODULAR SHOP UNITS. These units are the ultimate in home workshop design—allowing you to fit your own needs and space requirements.

FAMILY RECREATION WALL. There are many ways that your radial-arm machine can be housed. For example, it is possible to locate it in a family activity wall such as shown (above). Such a wall, which may be located in the basement, other family living areas such as a recreation room, or even in an apartment, contains built-in areas for three kinds of family hobby activities: a home shop (for you); a sewing center (for your wife); and a radio-TV-stereo-hi-fi center (for your children). When not in use, these areas are hidden behind attractive wall paneling (below).

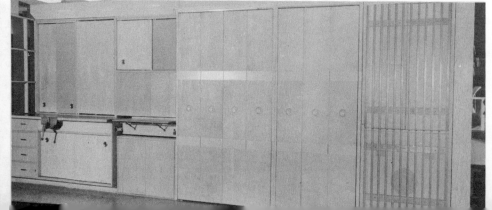

READER'S REFERENCE. To obtain further information on the various building materials mentioned here and in Chapter 10, as well as additional building project ideas, we suggest writing to the following manufacturers and associations:

Aluminum
Reynolds Metals Company, 6601 W. Broad St., Richmond, Va. 23218

Floor, Wall and Ceiling Coverings
Armstrong Cork Company, Liberty & Charlotte Sts., Lancaster, Pa. 17604
National Gypsum Company, 325 Delaware Ave., Buffalo, N.Y. 14202
United States Gypsum Company, 101 S. Wacker Dr., Chicago, Ill. 60606

Hardboard
Masonite Corporation, 29 N. Wacker Dr., Chicago, Ill. 60606

Hardware
Grant Pulley & Hardware Corporation, High St., W. Nyack, N.Y.

Honeycomb Panels
Johns-Manville Corporation, 22 E. 40th St., New York, N.Y. 10016
Koppers Company Inc., Koppers Bldg., Pittsburgh 19, Pa.

Laminated Plastic
Formica Company, 4514 Spring Grove Ave., Cincinnati, Ohio 45232

Plastics
Owens-Corning Fiberglas Corporation, National Bank Bldg., Toledo 1, Ohio

Plywood
American Plywood Association, 1119 A St., Tacoma, Wash. 98401
Hardwood Plywood Institute, 2310 S. Walter Reed Dr., Arlington 6, Va.

United States Plywood Corporation, 777 Third Ave., New York, N.Y. 10022

Wood and Lumber
California Redwood Association, 617 Montgomery St., San Francisco, Calif. 94111
National Lumber Manufacturers Association, 1619 Massachusetts Ave., N.W., Washington, D.C. 20036
Southern Pine Association, National Bank of Commerce Bldg., New Orleans 12, La.
Western Wood Products Association, 510 Yeon Bldg., Portland, Ore. 97204

Woodfinishing Materials
Deft, Incorporated, 612 Maple Ave., Torrance, Calif.
E. I. Du Pont de Nemours & Co., Inc., 1007 Market St., Wilmington, Del.
Sherwin-Williams Company, 101 Prospect Ave., N.W., Cleveland 1, Ohio
Weyerhaeuser Company, Tacoma Wash. 98401

General Information and Plans
Pamphlet #72 — Homes — Superintendent of Documents, Government Printing Office, Washington, D.C. 20402
Easi-Bild Pattern Co., Inc., Briarcliff Manor, N.Y.
Better Homes & Gardens, Des Moines, Iowa 50303
Books by John G. Shea, available from D. Van Nostrand Co., Inc., 120 Alexander St., Princeton, N.J. 08541 *(Woodworking for Everybody, Colonial Furniture Making for Everybody, Plywood Working for Everybody)*
Fifty-page reference booklet — eight basic plans with easy-to-build directions—available from The Black & Decker Manufacturing Company, Towson, Md. 21204. Send for Easy-to-Build Plan #677 (enclose 75¢ for Plan Booklet and mailing charges).

CHAPTER 13

CARE OF THE RADIAL-ARM MACHINE

ALIGNMENT PROCEDURE. All DeWalt machines are thoroughly tested, inspected and accurately adjusted before leaving the factory. Rough handling in shipment can, at times, affect adjustments. Because of this we recommend alignment check before operation. You will also find that because of overload and various excessive stresses and strains realignment and minor adjustments may periodically become necessary to maintain complete accuracy. Provisions are made for complete adjustment of all positions so that your DeWalt machine can be kept accurate for its entire life. A description of each of these adjustments follows and should be performed in the sequence listed.

NOTE: *The instructions which follow apply to the deluxe DeWalt. Operating instructions accompany other models, and should be referred to for the minor differences that occur.*

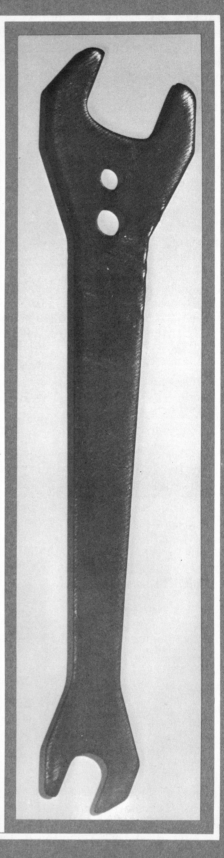

CHECK TABLE TOP AND GUIDE FENCE. The table top assembly and guide strip are checked for straightness with a master straight edge before leaving the factory. As all wood products must "breathe" and are affected by various humidity conditions, a slight change from factory conditions may sometimes be found. Straightness of top and guide strip, with clamp screws (at rear of table) tight, should be checked with a square or straight edge. Correction can be made only by sanding. A slight variation from perfect straightness of table top will not normally affect the average woodworking requirements. Do not use a level except as a straight edge. (This check is for straightness, not levelness with the floor.)

You may desire to place a hardboard or plywood protective top on the section of table top in front of the guide fence until you are more familiar with the operation of your machine. This procedure will eliminate excessive cutting into permanent top and, like the guide fence, is easily replaced when necessary. Be sure you countersink finishing nails and place them so as not to be in line with cutting tools.

Rip Scale. The rip scale is located on the right side of the radial arm. When the motor is positioned with motor arbor toward the column it is called in-rip position, and material should be fed from right to left. When the motor arbor is positioned toward the operator it is called out-rip and material is fed from left to right. When in-ripping width dimensions are located on the top of the scale and when out-ripping on the bottom of the scale by use of the reference pointers. The pointers are adjustable and must be readjusted only when gauge (thickness) of blade is changed. To adjust: *In-rip:* 1) Place the motor in in-rip and move the motor on the arm until the saw blade just touches the guide fence. 2) Loosen two screws on pointer base and move pointer until edge aligns with 0° on the top scale. Tighten back screw.

Out-rip: 1) Place a board of known width against the guide strip, position motor in out-rip position and move the motor until the blade just touches the material. 2) Loosen front screw only and move bottom pointer until the edge aligns with dimension on the lower scale of the known width of board. Tighten screw.

Miter Pointer. The miter pointer is located at the top in front of the arm. When the arm is positioned for straight cross-cut the pointer should be at 0° on the scale. Pointer can be moved horizontally for adjustment.

Bevel Scale. The bevel scale is located at the front of the motor. When the motor is positioned for vertical cutting the pointer should be at 0° on the scale. To adjust, loosen the two screws, move the pointer to 0°, and tighten.

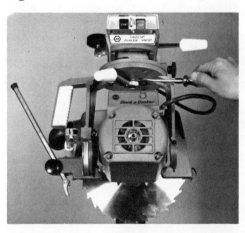

YOKE CLAMP HANDLE ADJUSTMENT. The purpose of this handle is to provide a friction lock between the upper face of the yoke and the bottom face of the rollerhead. It should also eliminate any play between these two parts. In operating position the yoke clamp handle is pushed back from the hand grip of the yoke. If at any time, it is possible to move this handle so that it strikes the rear leg of the yoke, it is not in proper adjustment. Its proper position for machine operation is approximately 90° or less to the hand grip of the yoke. To readjust: 1) Pull yoke clamp handle forward to release friction locking action. 2) Insert screw driver between the yoke and the notched clamp adjustor. Flex the adjustor downward just enough

to pass over the lug stop on the yoke. 3) Rotate clamp adjustor as necessary (to tighten, counter-clockwise; to loosen, clockwise). Be sure the notch in the adjustor is positioned properly over the yoke lug stop at final setting. If difficulty is encountered in making the above adjustment, we suggest that you remove the arm end cap and slide the entire motor, yoke, and rollerhead assemblies from the arm. This will provide access to the king bolt and by turning this with a screwdriver it will assist in the above adjustment procedure.

ADJUSTING BEVEL CLAMP HANDLE.

The purpose of the bevel clamp handle is to hold the motor at any angle. This is accomplished by the cam action of the clamp pulling the clamp pad against the dial plate. To adjust: Loosen set screw (A), tighten clamp bolt (B), then retighten set screw.

ADJUSTING ROLLERHEAD BEARINGS TO ARM TRACKS.

The rollerhead is suspended by four special-tolerance, grease-packed, double-shield ball bearings. These bearings are mounted on two straight bearing shafts and two eccentric bearing shafts. In proper adjustment the top and bottom radii of all four bearings should be in contact with the arm tracks for their entire length and head should roll freely. 1) Bring motor, yoke, and rollerhead assemblies to the end of arm. 2) Set in out-rip position. 3) Loosen hex nuts on left side, front and rear. 4) Insert socket wrench in recess at bottom of shafts and turn bearing shaft until the ball bearing touches the arm track on both top and bottom radii. Repeat for both eccentric shafts. CAUTION: Do not tighten too much. Bearings should only be sufficiently tightened so that they roll and do not slide. Be sure tracks are clean. 5) While holding each shaft in adjusted position, retighten the hex nuts.

REMOVING SHROUD.

To make adjustments in the arm it is necessary to remove the arm cover, as follows: 1) Unscrew arm clamp handle grip. 2) Remove elevating handle. Handle is held on by a set screw with a locking set screw on top of it. 3) Remove four screws holding plates on each side of arm. 4) Remove plates and arm cover.

ARM TO COLUMN. Prior to readjusting the arm clamp cam, check adjustment of the arm to column. With the arm clamp released there should be no vertical play in the arm, and arm should fit snugly on the column. To adjust: 1) Loosen two jam nuts (A) in slot at rear of arm, turning them clockwise. 2) Adjust bolts (B) for proper fit and retighten jam nuts (A).

ADJUSTING ARM CLAMP. The arm clamp handle operates a cam that clamps and releases the arm, and lifts the miter latch from the 0° and 45° slots. To adjust: 1) Loosen set screw (A) on clamp bolt (B) in clamp cam pivot pin (C). 2) To tighten clamp turn clamp bolt clockwise. (Very little adjustment should be made prior to trying the clamp.) 3) Retighten set screw (A) in clamp cam pivot pin (C) on the clamp bolt (B).

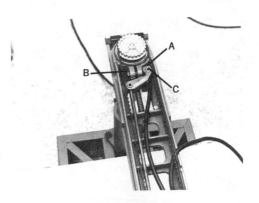

MITER CLAMP HANDLE POSITION. Position of the clamp handle may need adjusting after the clamp cam has been adjusted. To adjust: 1) Loosen set screw in pivot pin on the clamp rod. 2) Turn the clamp rod so that the handle does not contact casting when clamped or released. 3) Retighten set screw in pivot pin on the clamp rod.

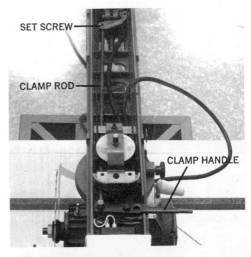

ADJUST BELT TENSION AND MITER SCALE TENSION. It is necessary to remove the arm cover to adjust the timing belt tension. To adjust: 1) Loosen two screws marked (A) and (B). 2) Pull and hold sprocket bracket (C) to apply belt tension. 3) Tighten screw (A). NOTE: When the belt tension is adjusted it is necessary to adjust the tension on the miter scale wire. 4) Pull and hold miter scale plate (D). 5) Tighten screw (B).

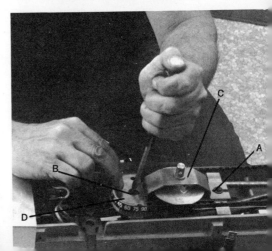

ADJUSTING BASE TO COLUMN. If, after the arm clamp handle is tightened, you have side motion at the end of the arm and this is caused by the column rotating in the base it indicates adjustment of the base is necessary. To adjust: (face rear of machine) 1) Loosen all base hardware above table frame level (6 pieces). There are: two pinch bolts (A) with lock nuts (top and bottom), two set screws (B) with lock nuts (top and bottom), and two set screws (C) without lock nuts (top and bottom). 2) Elevate and depress column. If base is too tight around the column causing binding tighten the small set screws (without lock nuts) until column moves freely. If base is not too tight leave these set screws loose. 3) Tighten the base pinch bolts (top and bottom) by turning the bolt heads on right side until the base fits snugly around the column diameter but column elevates and depresses freely.

Lock with nuts on left side. 4) To prevent side motion of the arm (rotation of column) tighten the top and bottom set screws against the column key. Be careful you do not tighten to the point of binding with resulting hindrance to the elevating. Lock by tightening jam nuts. 5) Tighten small set screws (the ones without lock nuts) at top of base if you have not already done so in 2) above.

ADJUSTING TABLE TOP PARALLEL WITH ARM. The table top surface must be parallel with the horizontal plane of the arm tracks. To check this alignment: 1) Insert the arbor nut wrench or a piece of steel about 10-inches long between the saw arbor collars. 2) Elevate or depress saw so that when swinging arbor wrench on the motor arbor the bottom of it just touches the table top. 3) Locate the highest spot on the table over adjusting cleats by moving arm on the column and the rollerhead along the arm tracks. 4) If the bottom of the arbor wrench in vertical position does not "just touch" the table top at all positions over the cleats adjustment is necessary. To readjust: 1) Remove and discard the four roll pins locking the cleats to the table frame. 2)

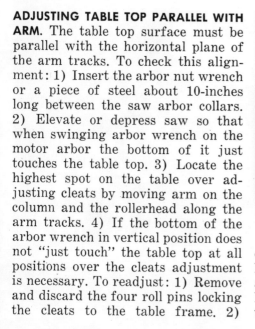

Loosen all locking nuts at the sides of the table frame except the one holding the highest point of the table as determined above. 3) Elevate the low sections to the same elevation as the highest and tighten all lock nuts.

ADJUSTING BLADE PERPENDICULAR TO WORK TOP. With the arm in cross-cut position, all latches engaged and all clamp handles locked place a steel square with one edge on the table top parallel to guide strip and the other edge against the flat of the saw blade (place in saw blade gullets and not

against teeth because of tooth set). If blade is not flat against square, adjust as follows: 1) Remove bevel pointer by removing two screws. 2) Loosen two outside socket head screws. 3) Tilt motor until blade is flat against the square and again lock (very firmly) socket head screws. Replace bevel pointer. NOTE: In some cases it will be found necessary to also loosen center cap screw in order to adjust motor.

ADJUSTING CROSS-CUT TRAVEL WITH GUIDE FENCE. With the miter latch engaged and arm clamp handle locked, place a wide board (1 inch by 12 inch if available) against the guide strip. Cross-cut this board with a set tooth blade. Check cut with a steel square. If cut is not square, the arm is out of alignment with the guide fence. To readjust: 1) Loosen arm clamp handle. 2) Loosen two set screws (A). 3) Lay steel square on table top with one edge against guide fence and the other angle at 0° cross-cut. 4) Move saw carriage and blade forward along steel square to determine which way arm must be adjusted. 5) If saw blade moves toward square as it comes forward, disengage miter latch. With screw driver loosen left adjusting screw and tighten right adjusting screw, re-engage miter latch. Check and repeat if necessary. 6) If saw blade moves away from square as it

comes forward, disengage miter latch. Loosen right adjusting screw and tighten left adjusting screw, reengage miter latch. Check and repeat if necessary. 7) When saw travel is parallel to square for entire length, lock adjustment screws in place by retightening set screws. NOTE: Do not tighten adjusting screws enough to retard the operation of the miter latch.

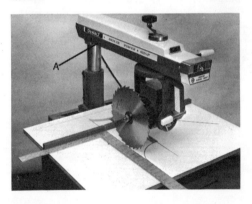

ADJUSTING CROSS-CUT TRAVEL PARALLEL TO ARM TRACKS. Both the leading and trailing teeth of the saw blade should travel in the same plane parallel to the arm tracks. To check, place a board 4 inch by 1 inch or larger against the right side of the guide fence. With the machine in 0° cross-cut position and all locks and latches engaged, end trim this stock by sliding to the right before returning the cutting head to the back of the arm. Examine the cut edge of the stock. If blade marks of the rear teeth are prominent on the cut stock, the rear teeth are not exactly following the front teeth and adjustment is necessary. (The arcs of the rear teeth

start at the bottom front of the stock and travel up and back.) Repeat this same operation with the stock against the left side of the guide fence. To adjust when marks are on stock cut on right side: 1) Disengage bevel clamp handle. Do not pull bevel pin. 2) Loosen right and left lock nuts at rear of yoke. 3) Loosen left set screw about 1/6 turn and tighten right set screw. 4) Retighten lock nuts and bevel clamp handle. 5) Recheck as above by cutting.

To adjust when marks are on stock cut on left side: 1) Disengage bevel clamp handle. Do not pull bevel pin. 2) Loosen right and left lock nuts. 3) Loosen right set screw about 1/6

cross-cut position and again make cuts on 2 inch by 4 inch stock as was done in cross-cut position. If tooth marks again appear the motor is too high or low in the rear of the yoke. To adjust when marks appear on bottom side of cut (left-hand piece of stock) : 1) Disengage bevel clamp handle. Do not pull bevel pin. 2) Loosen all lock nuts. 3) Loosen right set screws about 1/6 turn and tighten bottom set screw. 4) Retighten lock nuts and bevel clamp handle and recheck as above by cutting.

To adjust when marks appear on upper side of cut : 1) Disengage bevel clamp handle. Do not pull bevel pin. 2) Loosen all lock nuts. 3) Loosen bottom set screw about 1/6 turn and tighten right set screws. 4) Retighten lock nuts and bevel clamp handle and recheck as above by cutting.

turn and tighten left set screw. 4) Retighten lock nuts and bevel clamp handle. 5) Recheck as above by cutting.

After left and right adjustments have been made, tilt the motor to 45° bevel

ADJUSTING TABLE BOARD CLAMPS.
The back boards are clamped by the operation of the clamp cam in front of the table. To adjust: 1) Release table clamps. 2) Loosen lock nut. 3) Turn clamp rod clockwise to tighten and counter-clockwise to loosen. 4) When desired adjustment is obtained retighten lock nut. 5) Repeat on opposite side.

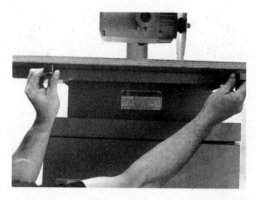

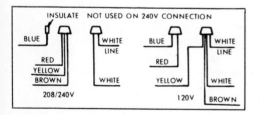

VOLTAGE CONNECTIONS FOR SINGLE PHASE. 1) The deluxe machine is equipped with a dual voltage motor 120/208-240V. 2) To change from originally connected voltage, remove specification plate, unscrew insulators, and reconnect as per diagram. a) Be careful not to exert any undue strain on wires or tamper with permanent solder connections. b) Connection marked "White Line" is the power supply line.

DIRECTIONS FOR REMOVING ARBOR NUT.

1. Fit 5/16" Allen wrench into front end of motor shaft. (This is a holding wrench only.)
2. Fit large wrench on arbor nut as

nearly parallel to first wrench as possible.
3. While holding first wrench stationary with left hand, use downward pressure of right hand on second wrench and nut will loosen.

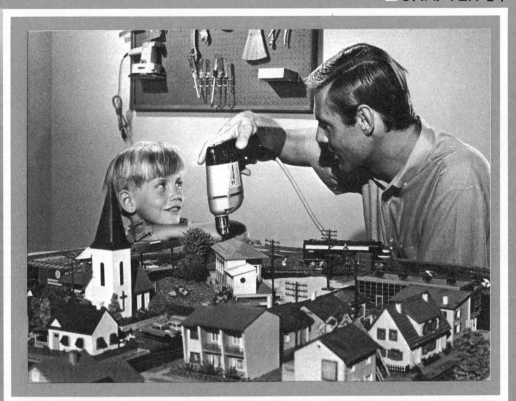

CHAPTER 14

PORTABLE POWER TOOLS SPEED PROJECTS TO COMPLETION

As you begin to assemble the pieces cut, shaped, dadoed or rabbetted with split-hair precision by the multi-purpose radial-arm machine, you suddenly find your skills limited only to what you can do with your hands. The project grows bigger; it's out of reach of the husky, versatile tool which, up to the point of assembly, made woodworking so easy.

Here's where a modest selection of portable power tools can take over to maintain the quality of craftsmanship by bringing power and precision to the work when the work can no longer be carried to the machine.

You'll find, too, that portable power tools can handle many operations to supplement the radial-arm machine. This doesn't mean that the acquisition of portable power tools will reduce the usefulness of the radial-arm machine. Far from it. The portables will round out your workshop and give you a choice of several ways to perform many operations. For example: when working alone in your shop, it's easier to rip a large plywood panel down the center by guiding a portable circular saw along a straight-edge clamped to the panel. But, on the other hand, crosscuts and angle cuts on long, unwieldy boards can be made more easily and with far greater accuracy beneath the rigid, calibrated overarm of the DeWalt.

Each new tool you add to your shop increases the flexibility, scope and quality of your work.

This short chapter couldn't possibly describe in detail all the operations you can perform with portable power tools; it would take an entire book to bring you that much information. The important thing here is how portable tools can *complement* the radial-arm machine and make your workshop complete for any hobby or home improvement.

START WITH A DRILL. Used with the wide variety of drill bits, spade bits, masonry bits and hole saws available, an electric drill can put clean holes of all sizes in wood, metal, plastic, concrete and brick. It makes short work of drilling pilot holes for screws, installing hardware, and setting masonry anchors or other expansion fasteners for hanging cabinets on basement or plaster walls.

Don't treat the purchase of a drill casually, however. Consider the job and materials. If you have heavier jobs, you'll want to use a double-reduction geared ⅜-inch drill. For

lighter work, use the ¼-inch. A quality drill will see plenty of use in your shop but a drill bought for its low price alone may prove constantly frustrating or stall out completely when you bear down to put a ½-inch hole in hardwood or try to drill through steel.

For complete mobility and freedom from extension cords, the cordless drill will handle drilling jobs with efficiency and convenience. Its self-contained power pack is shockproof and will accept over 400 recharges. It's completely enclosed and burn-out proof. It will drill several hundred holes before recharging is necessary. The cordless drill has been very popular with boating enthusiasts because of the added safety it offers.

Another recent development is the all-insulated drill which has a non-metallic housing and additional insulation around the motor. This tool is insulated inside and out to permit the use of a conventional two-prong plug. Adapters and grounding wires are eliminated.

HOLES UP TO 2½-INCH DIAMETER WITH ¼-INCH DRILL.

The ¼-inch drill is most popular with home craftsmen. Its chuck will take drill shanks up to ¼-inch diameter, but this doesn't mean that the largest hole it can drill is ¼-inch. Twist drills up to ½-inch size are available with shanks shouldered down to fit the ¼-inch chuck. Wood bits, called spade bits, have ¼-inch shanks to fit this popular tool, but the business end of these bits ranges in size from ⅜-inch to 1-inch. Their drilling depth is limited only by their length, provided the tool is held steady, pressed lightly into the wood, and pulled back occasionally while drilling to clear the hole of chips.

For really large holes, slip a ¼-inch arbor in the chuck and fasten a cup-like hole saw on its end. These rotary saws have teeth around their perim-

eter, come in sizes from ⅜-inch to 2½-inch diameter, and cut through material up to ¾-inch thick. A pilot bit locked in the arbor drills into the work first to center the hole on the mark and keep the saw from wobbling as it cuts. Using the pilot hole as a guide for drilling in from both sides, material up to 1½-inch thick can be drilled through. What easier way could you drill holes in joists so that water and heating pipes could be installed above the finished ceiling? Hole saws are perfect for precision jobs such as cutting the many holes of different sizes needed in the chassis of home-built radios or other electronic equipment, or for simpler but equally important jobs such as the entrance hole in a wren house.

Delicate drilling jobs with tiny drill bits thinner than a needle (sizes 61 to 80) are done best by locking the electric drill in a bench drill stand that converts it to an accurate drill press for a degree of drilling precision far beyond that obtained by hand-holding the tool. A lever applies light-feed pressure to minimize drill bit breakage, and an adjustable stop limits drilling depth for blind holes.

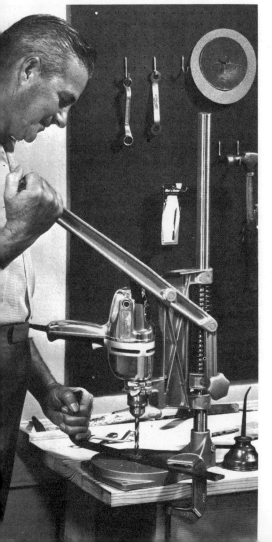

EQUIP YOUR DRILL FOR MAXIMUM USE.

Drilling holes is but one of many jobs you can do with an electric drill. Its husky motor can drive a wide variety of accessories designed to keep the tool constantly busy as a grinder, power wire brush, rotary polisher, disc sander, paint mixer—even a power screwdriver that will save hours of time and much arm fatigue if you ever decide to build a boat (it takes hundreds of screws to assemble a boat hull).

A right angle attachment permits drilling around corners or in cramped spaces where the drill could not be used perpendicular to the work surface.

Some of these useful accessories are simply locked in the drill chuck, others screw onto the spindle after removing the chuck. Either way requires only seconds to set up for work.

When such jobs as grinding tools, wire brushing, or polishing small objects require two hands to hold the work, the drill can be fixed securely in a horizontal bench stand. Pressing a button on the trigger switch locks to tool in the "ON" position; touching the trigger instantly turns the tool off.

Drill accessories can be added one at a time as you find the need for them, or you can get off to a good start and save some money, too, by purchasing a ¼-inch drill kit complete with many most-used accessories packed in a handy carrying case that you can tote from job to job. Good storage too!

PORTABLE CIRCULAR SAW TAKES OVER WHERE RADIAL-ARM SAW LEAVES OFF.

Suspending a circular saw on an overhanging arm, as Raymond DeWalt did in 1922, vastly increased its accuracy and versatility, but it did take away one thing—its portability. For that reason alone, there will always be a place in every shop for the portable circular saw.

Many projects require some cutting or trimming after or near completion. Take a tool chest or storage cabinet, for example. Many experts maintain that the best and easiest way to match the lid to the box is to build a completely-enclosed six-sided box, then cut about two or three inches from the top to free the lid. When hinged in place and fitted with catches, the lid matches the box perfectly, both in dimension and in the pattern of the grain. If the chest is fairly large, this operation can't be done with the radial-arm saw, but it's no trick at all to clamp a straightedge to each of the four sides of the box in turn and run a portable saw along it to cut the lid free. Note that all the parts for the box are easily cut to exact dimensions and rabbetted on the radial-arm saw, but the portable saw is needed to cut the lid free. This is a good example of the many ways a portable tool can

complement the radial-arm machine.

When framing a garage or an addition to your house, the radial arm saw is practically a necessity for cutting framing lumber square and to exact lengths. This is where the portable complements the radial-arm saw on the job. When you nail sheathing boards over the framing, with the ends hanging over the studs or rafters, you'll find it's easier to cut them off all at once, straight and true, with a portable saw.

A change of plan or belated improvement in a partly completed project could mean dismantling the job unless you're equipped with portable tools. Suppose, for example, after dadoing the sides of a bookcase for shelves, you assemble the bookcase and then decide to add partitions. Additional dado cuts can be made without taking the job apart simply by using a saw protractor or cutoff guide to run the saw at 90° across the shelves with the blade set for about 3/8-inch cutting depth. Repeated cuts are made until the desired dado width is obtained.

MATERIALS OTHER THAN WOOD can be cut readily by fitting the portable saw with the proper blade. An aluminum oxide abrasive disc will slice through steel rods, tubing, or sheet rock. A friction blade should be used on corrugated steel roofing and siding panels up to 16-gauge. These blades have toothlike notches, but they cut by heat generated as they are pressed against the material.

For cutting tile, brick, terrazzo, concrete, asbestos cement, marble, or slate for that new patio, a silicon carbide blade is right.

A carbide-tipped blade is the all-around tough blade for hardwood, plasterboard, hardboard, and asbestos cement board. It cuts fast and the hard carbide points stay sharp almost indefinitely under normal home-shop use. Always keep blades sharp.

SAW TABLE ADDS TO USEFULNESS OF PORTABLE SAW. No single tool or tool setup is the answer to all the problems in woodworking. Even though you have a radial-arm saw and a portable saw, there are some jobs that are done best on a table saw. Your portable saw can handle any table saw job by mounting it in an accessory saw table which comes complete with an adjustable rip fence that automatically aligns itself with the saw blade and a miter gauge for precision crosscuts at any angle. The same adjustments used for hand operation—bevel settings and depth of cut—are used to tilt the blade in the table or raise and lower it as required.

PORTABLE JIG SAW CAN ROAM OVER LARGE PIECES. As versatile as the saber saw is, its capacity is limited by the distance between the radial-arm column and the saw blade. While this gives considerable throat depth, the intricate scroll-work in a floor-to-ceiling Shoji screen, for example,

could not be cut with the stationary saber saw for two reasons: the long panel would strike the machine column as it was turned to follow the design, and the long panel would be difficult to maneuver in order to keep the blade on the cutting line. The portable jig saw is a compact handful of power that can follow a cutting pattern all the way to infinity, if that were possible.

Scrollwork is only one of many jobs you can do with a portable jig saw. By tilting it slowly into the work, it will start its own inside cut without drilling a starting hole. Use it to cut large openings for hi-fi speakers, and save the cut-out discs to make tops for garden tables. A jig saw is a must for devotees of early American furniture with its scalloped trim, valances and coves.

When the woodworking is finished and it's time to trim your project or upholster it, slip a special knife-edge blade in the jig saw for cutting leather, rubber, canvas, acoustical ceiling tile, heavy cardboard, composition board, and rubber or vinyl floor tile. Soft material such as cloth, suede leather, pigskin, or kid should be sandwiched between cardboard to keep it from wrinkling under the cutting knife.

Two useful accessories add to the basic usefulness of the jig saw; a circle-cutting guide, which swings the tool in an accurate arc around a pivot nail, and a rip guide for straight-line ripping of long pieces.

Some portable jig saws have a built-in quadrant graduated in degrees for cutting bevels. Any cut made at a square 90° angle can be cut on a bevel with just a bit more care, because the blade saws through more material when cutting on a slant than when sawing straight up and down. The newest jig saws have speed selection built in—high medium, and low speeds for different jobs and materials.

SANDERS SAVE ELBOW GREASE. Two tools that especially complement the radial-arm machine are the belt sander and the finishing sander. Sanding on the radial-arm machine is limited to disc and drum sanding—both primarily edge-smoothing operations —although the disc can be used flat for surfacing boards.

Portable sanders are used to smooth the surface of a completed project before applying the finish. Experts know that a finish is only as good as the surface over which it's applied; a scratch, dent, or gouge will show up as a scratch, dent, or gouge in the finish. Power sanding makes it easy to remove such surface imperfections.

THE BELT SANDER is a powerful finishing tool that will remove paint and smooth poorly-fitted joints until they are flush with the rest of the work. The belt rotates fast on two drumlike pulleys, and it works fast—so fast that the tool should be kept moving at all times to assure smooth, even finish. Heavy or light removal of material can be determined by proper selection of sanding belts.

Once the heavy sanding is done, the surface scratches can be smoothed by switching to medium then fine grit belts. Final sanding must be done by holding the belt sander parallel with the grain of the wood and moving it constantly back and forth.

THE FINISHING SANDER is most popular with the typical home workshopper who builds his projects carefully with new lumber. Only a modest amount of smoothing is needed to prepare mill-surfaced stock for finishing, and the orbital action of a finishing sander leaves the surface satin smooth.

Since the abrasive platen moves in a circular orbit only 3/16 inch in diameter, it doesn't matter how you hold the tool in relation to the wood grain. The platen extends beyond the body of the tool so that the sandpaper can do its work in corners or alongside vertical surfaces. As with any sanding operation—even hand sanding—best results are obtained by working over the surface with progressively finer paper of the open-coat type. The grit on this paper is widely spaced so that standing dust can't clog it and reduce the sanding action as quickly as on closed-coat paper.

Few home craftsmen are aware of the finishing sander's capability as a

polishing tool. The platen's circular motion duplicates on a smaller scale the uninterrupted motion used by French polishers to bring out a deep, glossy finish on fine cabinetwork.

To rub a finish or polish with the sander, stretch several layers of cloth over the platen and spread rubbing compound over the cloth. Move the sander lightly over a varnished or lacquered surface, keeping the compound wet with occasional drops of water. For large areas, it may be necessary to change the cloths and apply fresh compound several times.

Brush marks can be smoothed before polishing by clamping 600 grit wet-or-dry abrasive paper on the platen and wetting it with water while running lightly over the finish.

Sheet metal, too, can be given a satin sheen or a brilliant luster by polishing with coarse compound or polishing rouge applied to a cloth on the platen.

For ultra smoothness of straight-line sanding a combination orbital and straight-line sander is recommended.

DUST COLLECTORS KEEP THE HOUSE CLEAN. All your good work will get little appreciation if the fine dust created by sanding finds its way upstairs to settle on furniture and draperies. Keep peace in the family and do better work with a dust collector attachment that keeps the air clear and prevents dust from clogging the sandpaper. Your home vacuum cleaner can be fitted with an adapter

that snaps into a suction hole in the belt sander, or attaches to a dust-catching skirt slipped over the body of the finishing sander. Either type will pull better than 90 percent of the sanding dust into the bag, saving you hours of cleanup time in the shop. Also, you can get a Black & Decker dustless belt sander which has the dust collecting bag and water built in.

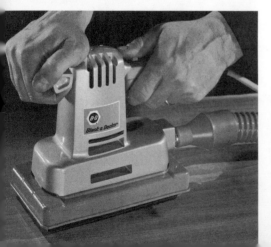

ROUTER IS A "MUST" FOR CABINET WORK. The Black & Decker heavy-duty router gets the popular vote as "the tool most likely to give amateur work a professional look."

The tool is designed for speed, accuracy, and simplicity of use in performing the finest joinery and the most beautiful cabinet work—beading, grooving, routing, fluting, cove-cutting, dovetailing, rabbetting, and mortising. With virtually no skill other than the ability to follow instructions and set up the tool carefully, you can do inlay work and bas-relief carving, cut decorative edges on unfinished boards or finished projects, or make your own molding from inexpensive lumber. The router even sharpens its own cutter bits, insuring smooth cuts that require little or no sanding prior to finishing.

The husky $7/8$-horsepower router motor drives the bits and cutters direct at speeds up to 21,000 r.p.m.

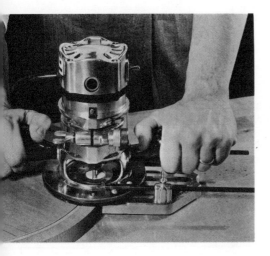

TYPICAL CUTS AND JOINTS

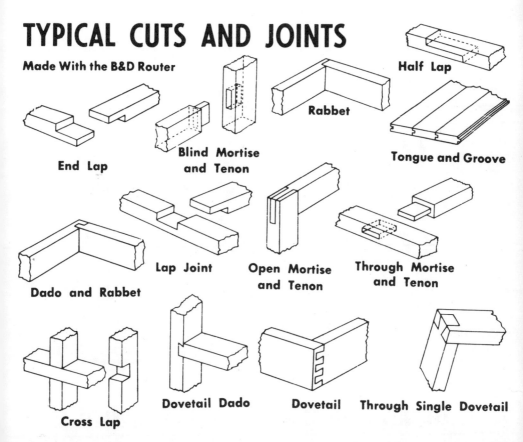

Made With the B&D Router

Half Lap

Rabbet

End Lap

Blind Mortise and Tenon

Tongue and Groove

Dado and Rabbet

Lap Joint

Open Mortise and Tenon

Through Mortise and Tenon

Cross Lap

Dovetail Dado

Dovetail

Through Single Dovetail

Before working with such a compact package of power, you should memorize these safety rules:

- Disconnect current when attaching or removing bits and cutters.
- Be sure that all adjustments are tight before operating router.
- Hold the tool firmly when turning it on to overcome starting torque of the motor.
- Don't attempt to make any adjustments while the tool is running.
- Clamp work being routed, or hold it securely in a fixture.
- Keep the base flat on material being cut and move the tool through the work from left to right fast enough to prevent burning, but not to the extent of overloading it.
- Keep fingers away from revolving cutters and bits.
- Keep bits and cutters sharp for clean cuts with a minimum of feed pressure.

ROUTER BITS

B & D Router Bits are made of selected hi-speed tool steel, carefully inspected and controlled for top quality. Only Black and Decker Bits and Cutters are recommended for use with the B & D Router.

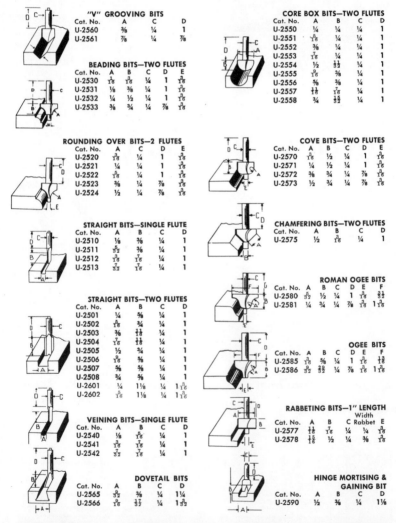

"V" GROOVING BITS

Cat. No.	A	C	D
U-2560	3/8	1/4	1
U-2561	7/8	1/4	7/8

BEADING BITS—TWO FLUTES

Cat. No.	A	B	C	D	E
U-2530	1/16	1/16	1/4	1	1/16
U-2531	1/8	3/8	1/4	1	1/16
U-2532	1/4	1/2	1/4	1	1/16
U-2533	3/8	3/4	1/4	7/8	3/16

ROUNDING OVER BITS—2 FLUTES

Cat. No.	A	C	D	E
U-2520	1/16	1/4	1	1/16
U-2521	1/4	1/4	1	1/16
U-2522	1/8	1/4	1	1/16
U-2523	3/8	1/4	7/8	3/16
U-2524	1/2	1/4	7/8	3/16

STRAIGHT BITS—SINGLE FLUTE

Cat. No.	A	B	C	D
U-2510	1/8	3/8	1/4	1
U-2511	3/32	3/8	1/4	1
U-2512	1/16	7/16	1/4	1
U-2513	3/32	7/16	1/4	1

STRAIGHT BITS—TWO FLUTES

Cat. No.	A	B	C	D
U-2501	1/4	5/8	1/4	1
U-2502	1/16	3/4	1/4	1
U-2503	3/8	11/16	1/4	1
U-2504	7/16	11/16	1/4	1
U-2505	1/2	3/4	1/4	1
U-2506	1/16	5/8	1/4	1
U-2507	5/8	5/8	1/4	1
U-2508	3/4	5/8	1/4	1
U-2601	1/4	1 1/8	1/4	1 3/16
U-2602	1/16	1 1/8	1/4	1 3/16

VEINING BITS—SINGLE FLUTE

Cat. No.	A	B	C	D
U-2540	1/8	7/16	1/4	1
U-2541	1/16	7/16	1/4	1
U-2542	3/32	7/16	1/4	1

DOVETAIL BITS

Cat. No.	A	B	C	D
U-2565	3/32	3/8	1/4	1 1/4
U-2566	1/16	9/32	1/4	1 3/32

CORE BOX BITS—TWO FLUTES

Cat. No.	A	B	C	D
U-2550	1/4	1/4	1/4	1
U-2551	1/16	1/4	1/4	1
U-2552	3/8	1/4	1/4	1
U-2553	1/16	1/4	1/4	1
U-2554	1/2	11/32	1/4	1
U-2555	1/16	3/8	1/4	1
U-2556	5/8	3/8	1/4	1
U-2557	11/16	1/16	1/4	1
U-2558	3/4	13/32	1/4	1

COVE BITS—TWO FLUTES

Cat. No.	A	B	C	D	E
U-2570	1/16	1/2	1/4	1	1/16
U-2571	1/4	1/2	1/4	1	1/16
U-2572	3/8	3/4	1/4	7/8	3/16
U-2573	1/2	3/4	1/4	7/8	3/16

CHAMFERING BITS—TWO FLUTES

Cat. No.	A	B	C	D
U-2575	1/2	3/16	1/4	1

ROMAN OGEE BITS

Cat. No.	A	B	C	D	E	F
U-2580	3/32	1/2	1/4	1	1/16	13/16
U-2581	1/4	3/4	1/4	7/8	3/16	1 1/16

OGEE BITS

Cat. No.	A	B	C	D	E	F
U-2585	1/16	5/8	1/4	1	1/16	13/16
U-2586	3/32	13/32	1/4	7/8	3/16	1 1/16

RABBETING BITS—1" LENGTH

Cat. No.	A	B	C Rabbet Width	E
U-2577	11/16	7/16	1/4	1/4	1/16
U-2578	11/16	1/2	1/4	3/8	1/16

HINGE MORTISING & GAINING BIT

Cat. No.	A	B	C	D
U-2590	1/2	3/8	1/4	1 1/8

KEEP BITS & CUTTERS SHARP for SPEED and ACCURACY!

ATTACHING BITS AND CUTTERS. The shank of the router bit or cutter arbor should be inserted in the collet-type chuck to a depth of at least ½-inch. Two wrenches are used to tighten the collet; one wrench holds the collar stationary, while the other turns the collet nut from right to left to tighten it securely. This nut is turned from left to right to release the bit.

Depth of cut is adjusted by a rack and pinion which moves the motor up or down in the base with aluminum against steel to avoid binding. With the router base on a flat surface, loosen the wing nut and turn the knurled knob until the bit just touches the surface. Tighten the wing nut and invert the tool so that it rests on the motor. Set the micrometer-type depth adjustment dial to zero, then loosen the wing nut and turn the knurled knob to the desired depth of cut. The scale provides depth graduations in 64ths of an inch, permitting direct setting up to 1-inch without measuring the depth of the bit below the base. Attach and set the proper fixture or guide attachment to the base and the tool is ready for work. Complete and detailed instructions for mounting and adjustment are furnished with each router attachment.

ROUTER CUTTERS

These cutters enable many unique shaping operations to be performed. Place cutters singly, or in combination, on No. U-2430 Arbor and fit Arbor into Router chuck.

← No. U-2430 Arbor for B&D Cutters.

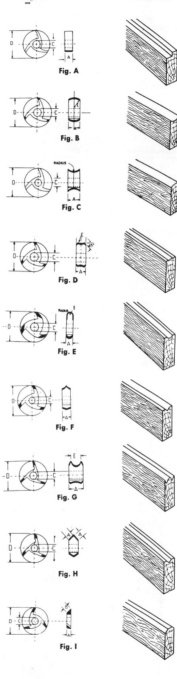

Fig. A

Fig. B

Fig. C

Fig. D

Fig. E

Fig. F

Fig. G

Fig. H

Fig. I

Fig. J

GUIDING THE ROUTER ALONG STRAIGHT EDGES. For rabbets or decorative cuts in straight edges, the adjustable guide is used with its straight edge attached. A vernier-type adjustment device permits precise setting of the lateral cutting depth in relation to the edge of the router bit or cutter. Once set and locked, the guide is pressed firmly against the work while the tool is moved along to make the cut.

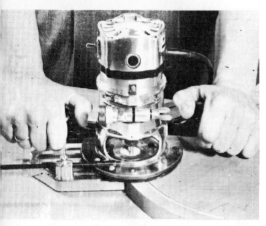

GUIDING THE TOOL ON CURVED EDGES. To move the tool accurately along curved edges or round work, the straight edge is removed from the guide, leaving two points of contact, one on each side of the cutter. As with straight cuts, the guide is pressed firmly against the work while the tool is moved along.

T-SQUARE GUIDES CROSS CUTS. A home made T-square can easily be assembled from scrap lumber to guide the router on cuts across the grain. Clamp the T-square to the work and guide the base of the tool along its edge.

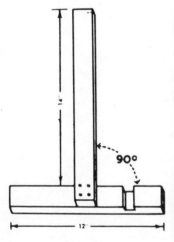

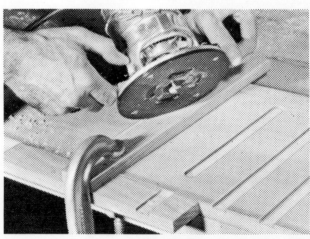

CUTTING CIRCLES WITH THE ROUTER.
The slot and circle cutting attachment includes a pivot pin for guiding the router in a circular motion, and a guide bar for cutting parallel grooves. With the pin set in a predrilled ¼-inch hole, the router is moved in a counter-clockwise direction to cut wheels or flat disks out of lumber. A piece of scrap placed beneath the work prevents the tool from cutting through to the workbench.

ROUTING CIRCULAR DESIGNS.
Interesting circular designs in round or square blocks can be made by swinging the tool on the pivot pin with the bit set for shallow cutting. Combining bits of several types creates artistic rosettes for use on mantles and door trim.

After routing the design, a straight router bit can be used to cut it out of the board, either by cutting a circle around the design, or by making straight cuts to remove a square block with the design centered in it.

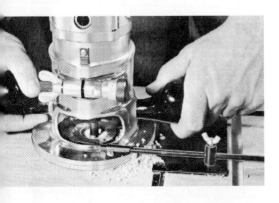

CUTTING GROOVES AND SLOTS.
With the pivot pin removed and a guide bar installed in its place, the attachment serves as a guide for cutting parallel grooves or slots. The first groove is cut by running the guide bar along the edge of the work, successive grooves by running the guide bar in the groove previously cut. Distance between the grooves can be varied by loosening the wing nuts and adjusting the attachment.

TEMPLATES SPEED INTRICATE ROUTING JOBS. The easiest method of duplicating intricate shapes is by using template guides to follow a pattern or template and to guide the router through identical movements.

Dovetails can be cut with speed and accuracy far beyond that achieved by hand cutting, using the dovetail templates and guides included in the Black & Decker dovetail kit. The two pieces to be joined are placed at right angles to each other and clamped. The male and female dovetails are cut in the edges of both boards at the same time, insuring a perfect fit.

When a design or scrollwork pattern must be duplicated several times, as when making dividers for a wall shelf, the design should be cut or routed freehand in plywood or hardboard to make a template. Tack the template to the piece to be routed and place it on a piece of scrap lumber to protect the bench top. Adjust the depth of cut to about one third the thickness of the material and lower the revolving bit into it. Move the router around, keeping the guide against the template until the area is completely cut out. Repeat in other areas of the pattern.

If the template is removed after the first pass, the design will appear in bas-relief. If the design is to be cut through the work, leave the template in place, adjust for a deeper cut and repeat the routing operation. Usually several passes are required to cut smoothly through the material.

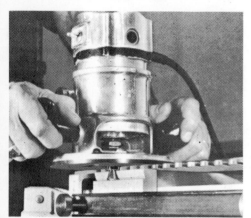

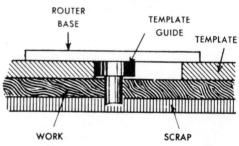

ROUTER BASE — TEMPLATE GUIDE — TEMPLATE — WORK — SCRAP

ATTACHMENT CONVERTS ROUTER TO PLANE. By mounting a sharp, helical cutter on the arbor and locking the router motor in the B&D planing attachment, you can edge-plane lumber to a smooth finish or remove excess material from doors to fit them quickly in their openings. Planing cuts up to 3/32 inch can be made, although the recommended cutting depth for most jobs is 1/32 inch with the 2⅛-inch cutter. The vertical guide on the plane attachment is adjustable for square or bevel planing.

Start planing with downward pressure on the front shoe of the attachment, then shift equal pressure to both hands while keeping the vertical guide firmly against the face of the work to maintain the planing angle. On nearing the end of the cut, transfer pressure to the right hand to hold the rear shoe firmly against the edge as the plane slides off the end of the work.

174

SHOP SAFETY

Safety is an important consideration in any shop, and certain safety rules should be stressed. The first one is to be sure that everyone working with hand or power tools is shop oriented—that he knows his way around your shop. Invite the entire family to join you in the planning and building of projects, but be sure you supervise their activity, especially when youngsters are involved.

The following list of safety hints will help you toward making your shop a center for more family enjoyment and woodworking pleasure.

DON'T forget, shop safety is a state of mind. Always think before doing. This stops accidents before they happen.

DON'T wear a necktie or loose-fitting clothes in your shop.

DON'T clutter the work surface of machines or work-bench with unnecessary objects.

DON'T operate tools that are not guarded properly.

DON'T fail to ground power tools.

DON'T use cracked saw blades or defective cutting tools on equipment.

DON'T allow your shop to become cluttered. Good housekeeping is essential.

DON'T permit horseplay in the shop. Invite the family to join you in home projects, but stress safety attitudes and business-like performance.

DON'T work around equipment when you are fatigued. Be alert.

DON'T permit shop tools, paints, thinners, etc., to get within reach of children.

DON'T leave a machine idling when not in actual use.

DON'T attempt to stop saw blades or cutting tools by forcing a piece of wood against, or into, it.

Special Safety Hints for Radial-Arm Power Tools:

DON'T leave safety key in machine when not in use.

DON'T start to cut unless motor and yoke are safely behind the guide fence.

DON'T rip unless the guard and anti-kickback device are set. Be sure you feed material from the end indicated on guard.

DON'T force the cut. Let the machine do the work. Use steady light pull for cross-cutting, a firm steady push for ripping.

DON'T forget that the motor rotation is clockwise, down and back, away from you. Mount all tools accordingly.

DON'T rip or shape close to saw blade or cutting tool unless a pusher stick is used.

Radial-arm equipment offer you these ten safety firsts:

- top side cutting
- layout marks in full view
- safety key switch
- push button control
- all controls above the table
- totally enclosed motor
- built-in automatic brake
- easy-to-read guides and scales
- guards that completely enclose the cutting tools
- space-saving, along-the-wall operation and location

VALUABLE INFORMATION FOR THE HOME SHOP

CHART OF GRADE REFERENCE FOR BUYING SOFTWOODS

SELECT: Lumber of good appearance and finishing qualities

SUITABLE FOR NATURAL FINISHES:

Grade A Practically free from defects

Grade B Allows a few small defects and blemishes

SUITABLE FOR PAINT FINISHES:

Grade C Allows a limited number of small defects or blemishes that can be covered with paint

Grade D Allows any number of defects or blemishes which do not detract from a finish appearance, especially when painted

COMMON: Lumber containing defects or blemishes which detract from a finish appearance, but which is suitable for general utility and constructional use.

LUMBER SUITABLE FOR USE WITHOUT WASTE:

No. 1 Common A sound and tight knotted stock. Size of defects and blemishes limited. May be considered watertight lumber.

No. 2 Common Allows large and coarse defects. May be considered graintight lumber.

LUMBER PERMITTING WASTE:

No. 3 Common Allows larger and coarser defects than No. 2 and occasional knotholes

No. 4 Common Low-quality lumber admitting the coarsest defects, such as decay and holes

No. 5 Common Must hold together under ordinary handling

NOMINAL AND ACTUAL SIZES OF LUMBER (Inches)

Nominal thickness	Softwood	Hardwood	Nominal width	Average actual width	
	Average actual thickness				
½	⁷⁄₁₆	½	1	²⁵⁄₃₂	⅞
1	²⁵⁄₃₂	⅞	2	1⅝	Usually sold
1¼	1⅛	1⅛	3	2⅝	to nearest
1½	1⁵⁄₁₆	1⅜	4	3⅝	nominal
1¾	1½	1⅝	6	5⅝	size at ran-
2	1⅝	1¾	8	7½	dom widths
3	2⅝	2¾	10	9½	with edges
			12	11½	left rough

BUFFING CHART

BUFFING COMPOUND	MATERIALS USED ON
White Rouge	For buffing chromium; aluminum, stainless steel, and cast brass.
Red Rouge	For buffing glass, gold, silver, and other precious metals to high luster.
Emery	For sharp cutting; removing rust, scale, tarnish, etc.
Tripoli	For buffing aluminum, brass, pewter, copper, wood, painted surfaces, plastic, animal horn, and hard rubber.

HARDWOOD GRADES
General grading—Indicates decrease in quality

HARDWOODS	1st AND 2d GRADES	3d GRADE	4th GRADE	5th GRADE	6th GRADE
Alder, ash, beech, birch, maple, oak, sycamore	Firsts and seconds	Selects	No. 1 Common	No. 2 Common	Sound Wormy
Cherry	Firsts and seconds	Selects	No. 1 Common	No. 2 Common	No. 3A Common
Chestnut	Firsts and seconds	Selects	No. 1 Common	Sound Wormy	No. 2 Common
Elm, hickory	Firsts and seconds	No. 1 Common	No. 2 Common	No. 3A Common	No. 3B Common
Mahogany, walnut	Firsts and seconds	Selects	No. 1 Common	No. 2 Common	No. 3 Common
Poplar	Firsts and seconds	Saps	Selects	Stained saps	No. 1 Common

FIRSTS: 91$\frac{2}{3}$ per cent clear both sides
SECONDS: 83$\frac{1}{3}$ per cent clear both sides
FIRSTS AND SECONDS: Not less than 20 per cent firsts (best commercial grade)
SELECTS: 90 per cent clear one side

NO. 1 COMMON: 66$\frac{2}{3}$ per cent clear face
NO. 2 COMMON: 50 per cent clear face
NO. 3A COMMON: 33$\frac{1}{3}$ per cent clear face
NO. 3B COMMON: 25 per cent clear face
SOUND WORMY: No. 1 Common with wormholes

HARDWOOD PLYWOOD STANDARD GRADES
(Commercial Standard 35-49)

GRADE	FACE VENEER	ALLOWABLE DEFECTS	GRADE	FACE VENEER	ALLOWABLE DEFECTS
1	Good Matched for pleasing effect	Burls, pin knots, mineral streaks, discolorations, and patches in limited amounts	3	Generally sound (with some cutting and/or repairs)	Same as grades 1 and 2 plus sound knots up to ¾ inch, open knots up to ⅜ inch, wormholes up to ⅛ inch, and splits
2	Good Unmatched	Same as grade 1, plus filled wormholes, pin wormholes, and open joints not exceeding 1/64 inch	4	Reject	May contain any type and number of defects which do not destroy the strength and serviceability of the veneer for backs, crating, etc.

GRADES OF EXTERIOR-TYPE DOUGLAS-FIR PLYWOOD*

GRADE AND REG. TRADE-MARK	FACE	BACK	WIDTH,† FEET	LENGTH,† FEET	THICKNESS,† INCHES
EXT-DFPA A-A	A	A	2½, 3, 3½, 4	5, 6, 7, 8, 9, 10, 12	³⁄₁₆, ¼, ³⁄₈, ½, ⅝, ¾, ⅞, 1, 1⅛
EXT-DFPA A-B	A	B	2½, 3, 3½, 4	5, 6, 7, 8, 9, 10, 12	³⁄₁₆, ¼, ³⁄₈, ½, ⅝, ¾, ⅞, 1, 1⅛
EXT-DFPA Plyshield	A	C	2½, 3, 3½, 4	5, 6, 7, 8, 9, 10, 12	³⁄₁₆, ¼, ³⁄₈, ½, ⅝, ¾, ⅞, 1, 1⅛
EXT-DFPA Utility	B	C	2½, 3, 3½, 4	5, 6, 7, 8, 9, 10, 12	³⁄₁₆, ¼, ³⁄₈, ½, ⅝, ¾, ⅞, 1, 1⅛
EXT-DFPA Sheathing	C	C	4	8, 9, 10, 12	⁵⁄₁₆, ³⁄₈, ½, ⅝
EXT-DFPA Plyform	B	B	4	8	⅝, ¾

GRADES OF INTERIOR-TYPE DOUGLAS-FIR PLYWOOD*

GRADE AND REG. TRADE-MARK	FACE	BACK	WIDTH,† FEET	LENGTH,† FEET	THICKNESS,† INCHES
Interior A-A	A	A	2½, 3, 3½, 4	5, 6, 7, 8, 9, 10, 12	³⁄₁₆, ¼, ³⁄₈, ½, ⅝, ¾
Interior A-B	A	B	2½, 3	5, 6, 7, 8, 9, 10, 12	³⁄₁₆, ¼, ³⁄₈, ½, ⅝, ¾
Plypanel	A	D	2½, 3,	5, 6, 7, 8, 9, 10, 12	³⁄₁₆, ¼, ³⁄₈, ½, ⅝, ¾
Plyscord	C	D	2½, 3, 3½, 4	8, 9, 10, 12	⁵⁄₁₆, ³⁄₈, ½, ⅝
Interior	B	B	4	8	¼, ½, ⁹⁄₁₆, ⅝, ¾

* All grades are sanded both sides except EXT—DFPA sheathing and Interior Plyscord, which are unsanded; ⅜-inch and thinner panels have a minimum of three plies; ½- to ¾-inch are five-ply minimum, ⅞-inch and thicker are seven-ply minimum.

† About three-fourths of all fir plywood is of panels 4 by 8 feet; all sizes shown are standard, but the volume of panels of dimensions other than 4 by 8 feet is small. The great majority of fir plywood is of panels ¼ to ¾ inch thick.

GENERAL WOOD-CHARACTERISTIC AND FINISHING CHART*

WOOD	NATURAL COLOR	GRAIN FIGURE	STAIN Type	STAIN Color	FILLER Weight[1]	FILLER Color	NATURAL FINISH	BLEACH	PAINT
Alder	Pink to brown	Plain or figured	Oil or water	Red or brown	None	None	Yes	Yes	Yes
Amaranth	Purple	Plain or stripe	None	None	8	Match wood	Yes	No	No
Ash	White to brown	Plain	Any	Any	1.5 to 2	White or brown	Yes	Yes	Yes
Aspen	Light straw	Plain or stripe	Water	Amber	None	None	Yes	No	Yes
Avodire	White to cream	Stripe	None	None	8	Match wood	Yes	Yes[2]	No
Basswood	Cream	Mild	Water	Red or brown	None	None	No	Yes[2]	Yes
Beech	White to brown	Mild	Water	Red or brown	8	Red or brown	No	Yes	Yes
Birch	Cream	Mild	Any	Walnut or mahogany	None or 7	Natural or brown	Yes	Yes	Yes
Bubinga	Pale red to flesh red	Plain to figured	Water	Red or brown	12 to 14	Red or brown	Yes	No	No
Butternut	Amber and cream	Like walnut	Water	Walnut or oak	12 to 14	Medium brown	Yes	Yes	No
Cedar	Red and cream	Knotty or stripe	None	None	None	None	Yes	No	No
Cherry	Red to brown	Fine	Water	Red or brown	6 to 8	Brown, red, or black	Yes	No	No
Chestnut	Gray-brown	Heavy grain	Oil[3]	Red or brown	15	Red or brown	Yes	Yes	Yes
Cypress	Brown and cream	Plain or figured	Water or oil[3]	Red or brown	None	None	Yes	No	Yes
Ebony	Dark brown to black	Plain or stripe	Water	Red or brown	None	None	Yes	No	No
Elm	Cream to brown	Heavy grain	Water	Red or brown	12 to 14	Dark brown	Yes	No	Yes
Fir (Douglas)	Cream	Wild	Oil[3]	Brown	None	None	No	No	Yes
Gaboon	Golden to pinkish tan	Plain or stripe	Water	Red or brown	None	None	Yes	No	No
Gum (red)	Cream and red	Plain or figured	Any	Red or brown	None or 4 to 6	Match wood	Yes	Yes	Yes
Hemlock	Light reddish brown	Plain	Water or oil[3]	Red or brown	None	None	No	No	Yes
Hickory	White to cream	Straight	Water	Red or brown	15	Brown	Yes	Yes	No
Holly	White	Mild	Water	Amber	None	None	Yes	Yes[2]	Yes
Kelobra	Brown	Plain or stripe	Water	Dark brown	12 to 14	Dark brown	Yes	Yes	No
Korina	Creamy gray	Plain or stripe	Water	Red or brown	12 to 14	Red or brown	Yes	Yes	No
Lacewood	Medium brown	Flake	Water	Oak	12 to 14	Dark brown	Yes	Yes	No
Locust	Golden brown	Wild	Water or oil	Brown	12 to 16	Brown	Yes	No	Yes

GENERAL WOOD-CHARACTERISTIC AND FINISHING CHART*

WOOD	NATURAL COLOR	GRAIN FIGURE	STAIN Type	STAIN Color	FILLER Weight[1]	FILLER Color	NATURAL FINISH	BLEACH	PAINT
Magnolia	Light to dark yellowish brown	Plain	Water or oil[3]	Brown	None	None	Yes	Yes	Yes
Mahogany	Brown to red-brown	Stripe	Water	Red or brown	12	Red, brown, or black	Yes	Yes	No
Mahogany (Philippine)	Brown to red-brown	Stripe	Water or oil[3]	Red or brown	18	Red, brown, or black	Yes	Yes	No
Maple	Cream	Varied	Water or oil[3]	Maple	None	None	Yes	Yes	Yes
Oak (red)	Red to brown	Plain or flake	Water	Light green	15	Brown	No	Yes	Yes
Oak (white)	White to pale brown	Plain or flake	Water	Brown	15	Brown	Yes	Yes	Yes
Orientalwood	Light brown	Stripe	Water	Amber or brown	12	Brown	Yes	No	No
Padouk	Golden red to deep crimson	Stripe or mottle	None	None	14 to 16	Red or brown	Yes	No	No
Pine (white)	White to cream	Very mild	Water or oil	Brown	None	None	No	No	Yes
Pine (yellow)	Cream to brown	Mild	Water or oil	Brown	None	None	Yes	No	Yes
Poplar	White	Mild	Water or oil[3]	Red or brown	None	None	No	No	Yes
Prima Vera	White to yellow	Stripe	Water	Amber	12	Natural	Yes	Yes	No
Redwood	Red	Mild	Oil[3]	Red	None	None	Yes	No	Yes
Rosewood	Red to brown	Stripe to varied	Water	Red	12 to 15	Dark red to black	Yes	Yes	No
Sapeli	Medium brown	Stripe	Water	Red or brown	10	Dark brown	Yes	Yes	No
Spruce	White	Plain	Water or oil[3]	Amber or brown	None	None	No	No	Yes
Sycamore	White to pink	Flake	Water	Amber or brown	None	None	Yes	Yes[2]	Yes
Teakwood	Golden brown	Plain or figured	Water or oil	Brown	16	Natural or brown	Yes	Yes	No
Tigerwood	Golden brown	Stripe	Water	Dark brown	8 to 12	Dark brown	Yes	Yes	No
Tupelo	Pale to brownish gray	Plain	Water	Brown	None to 7	Brown	Yes	Yes	Yes
Walnut	Cream and dark brown	Varied	Water	Dark brown	12 to 15	Brown to black	Yes	Yes	No
Zebrawood	Tan with brown stripe	Heavy stripe	Water	Light oak	12	Natural	Yes	No	No

* This chart is a general one and gives only the usual accepted finishes and uses of the wood.
[1] Weight designates number of pounds of filler plastic per gallon of thinner.
[2] Generally not necessary because of the light color of the wood.
[3] Penetrating oil stain may also be used. Non-grain-raising stains may be substituted for water stain through-out.

COMMON HOME-WORKSHOP WOODS*

NAME OF WOOD	HARDNESS	STRENGTH	STABILITY	WEIGHT	ROT RESISTANCE	SPLIT RESISTANCE	WORKING QUALITY FOR HAND TOOLS	SHAPING	TURNING	MORTISING	PLANING AND JOINTING	NAILING	GLUING	SANDING	REMARKS
Alder	Med.	Weak	G	Light	F	F	G	F	F	F	G	G	G	F	A Pacific Coast favorite
Ash	Med.	Med.	E	Med. heavy	F	G	P	E	F	F	G	G	F	E	Interior trim, tool handles; wears well
Basswood	Soft	Weak	G	Light	P	E	E	P	P	F	G	E	E	P	Used as core stock
Beech	Hard	Med.	P	Heavy	P	G	F	F	F	G	F	P	G	G	Not durable outside; hard on hand tools
Birch	Hard	Strong	G	Heavy	F	G	P	E	G	E	G	P	F	F	Fine furniture, trim, flooring, and veneers
Butternut	Soft	Weak	E	Light	F	F	G	F	G	F	G	F	G	F	Furniture, sometimes called "White Walnut"
Cedar	Soft	Weak	G	Med.	E	P	G	P	P	F	F	P	G	P	Trim, chest lining, outside use
Cherry	Med.	Med.	G	Heavy	F	P	G	E	E	E	E	F	E	E	Furniture, joiner work, novelties
Chestnut	Soft	Weak	E	Light	E	P	G	G	E	G	G	G	E	E	Scarce; fine for turning
Cypress	Soft	Med.	G	Med.	E	F	F	P	P	P	G	F	F	F	Excellent for outdoor use
Elm	Med.	Med.	P	Med. heavy	F	G	F	P	P	G	P	E	F	G	Bends well; very durable under paint
Fir (Douglas)	Med.	Med. strong	F	Med. heavy	G	F	F	P	P	G	G	G	G	F	Common plywood veneer
Gum, red	Med.	Med.	P	Med.	F	G	G	F	E	F	F	G	E	F	Furniture; substitute for mahogany and walnut
Hickory	Hard	Strong	G	Heavy	P	F	P	F	G	E	G	P	G	E	Bends easily; furniture and sports equipment
Magnolia	Soft	Weak	F	Med.	F	G	G	G	F	P	G	E	E	G	Bends easily
Mahogany	Med.	Med.	E	Med. heavy	F	P	G	E	E	E	G	G	E	G	Excellent furniture wood and boats
Mahogany Philippine	Med.	Med.	E	Med.	G	P	G	F	G	F	G	G	E	P	Furniture and boats
Maple, hard	Hard	Strong	G	Heavy	P	P	F	E	E	E	F	P	F	G	Excellent furniture wood, flooring, trim, fine for turning
Maple, soft	Med.	Med.	F	Med.	F	G	G	F	F	P	P	F	G	G	Difficult to machine smooth
Oak, red	Hard	Strong	E	Heavy	P	F	P	F	G	E	E	G	G	E	Substitute for white oak in less expensive work
Oak, white	Hard	Strong	E	Heavy	F	F	P	G	G	E	E	G	G	E	Excellent furniture wood, flooring, trim
Pine, white	Soft	Weak	G	Light	F	P	E	G	G	F	G	E	E	G	Best all-around soft wood
Pine, yellow	Hard	Strong	F	Heavy	G	P	F	G	P	G	G	F	F	F	Carpentry work
Poplar	Soft	Weak	G	Med.	P	G	E	P	G	F	G	E	E	P	Good for toys and carving
Redwood	Soft	Med.	E	Med.	E	G	G	G	F	P	G	G	E	P	Excellent for outdoor and indoor use
Sycamore	Med.	Med.	P	Heavy	F	G	G	P	G	E	P	E	G	P	Furniture and trim
Walnut	Med.	Strong	E	Heavy	G	F	G	G	E	E	G	F	E	E	Excellent for furniture, cabinetwork, trim

*E = excellent, G = good, F = fair, P = poor.

LUMBER CALCULATOR — BOARD FEET FOR VARIOUS LENGTHS

Size in inches			8-foot	10-foot	12-foot	14-foot	16-foot
1	×	2	1⅓	1⅔	2	2⅓	2⅔
1	×	3	2	2½	3	3½	4
1	×	4	2⅔	3⅓	4	4⅔	5⅓
1	×	5	3⅓	4⅙	5	5⅚	6⅔
1	×	6	4	5	6	7	8
1	×	8	5⅓	6⅔	8	9⅓	10⅔
1	×	10	6⅔	8½	10	11⅔	13⅓
1	×	12	8	10	12	14	16
1¼ *	×	4	3⅓	4⅙	5	5⅚	6⅔
1¼ *	×	6	5	6¼	7½	8¾	10
1¼ *	×	8	6⅔	8⅓	10	11⅔	13⅓
1¼ *	×	10	8⅓	10⁵⁄₁₂	12½	14⁷⁄₁₂	16⅔
1¼ *	×	12	10	12½	15	17½	20
2	×	4	5⅓	6⅔	8	9⅓	10⅔
2	×	6	8	10	12	14	16
2	×	8	10⅔	13⅓	16	18⅔	21⅓
2	×	10	13⅓	16⅔	20	23⅓	26⅔
2	×	12	16	20	24	28	32

* Sometimes referred to as five-quarter boards.

COMPARISON OF GLUES

	ANIMAL GLUE	LIQUID GLUE	CASEIN GLUE	UREA RESIN GLUE	RESORANAL GLUE	CONTACT GLUE
Ready mixed	Both	Yes	No	No	No	Yes
Resists dampness	No	Yes	Yes	Yes	Yes	Yes
Water-proof	No	Yes	No	Yes	Yes	Yes
Stains	Yes	No	Stains certain woods	No	Yes	No
Pressure needed	Heavy	Slight	Medium	Heavy	Medium	None
Drying time	2-4 hr.	10-30 min.	4-5 hr.	3-6 hr.	4-10 hr.	1 hr.
Setting temperatures	Any above freezing	Any above freezing	Any above freezing	70° F. up	70° F. up	70° F. up
Gap filling	Yes	No	Yes	Yes	Yes	No
Special uses	General indoors	Repairs small articles	Heavy work. Oily wood. Furniture	Veneers. Furniture	Outdoor work. Oily wood	For holding laminated plastic
Home craftsman	Harder to use than most types	Handy for small jobs and quick applications	Easy to use Long lasting	Easy to use	Fairly easy to use. Waterproof	Easy to use, but manufacturer's instructions must be followed

SCREW CHART—DRILL AND BIT SIZES

SIZE OF SCREW	BIT OR DRILL SIZES						AUGER BIT FOR COUNTER-SINK (By 16ths)
	SHANK HOLES		PILOT HOLES				
			Hard Wood		Soft Wood		
	DRILL NUMBER OR LETTER	DRILL SIZE NEAREST FRACTION	DRILL NUMBER OR LETTER	DRILL SIZE NEAREST FRACTION	DRILL NUMBER OR LETTER	DRILL SIZE NEAREST FRACTION	
0	52	1/16″	70	1/32″	75	1/64″	—
1	47	5/64″	66	1/32″	71	1/32″	—
2	42	3/32″	56	3/64″	65	1/32″	3
3	37	7/64″	54	1/16″	58	3/64″	4
4	32	7/64″	52	1/16″	55	3/64″	4
5	30	1/8″	49	5/64″	53	1/16″	4
6	27	9/64″	47	5/64″	52	1/16″	5
7	22	5/32″	44	3/32″	51	1/16″	5
8	18	11/64″	40	3/32″	48	5/64″	6
9	14	3/16″	37	7/64″	45	5/64″	6
10	10	3/16″	33	7/64″	43	3/32″	6
11	4	13/64″	31	1/8″	40	3/32″	7
12	2	7/32″	30	1/8″	38	7/64″	7
14	D	1/4″	25	9/64″	32	7/64″	8
16	I	17/64″	18	5/32″	29	9/64″	9
18	N	19/64″	13	3/16″	26	9/64″	10
20	P	21/64″	4	13/64″	19	11/64″	11
24	V	3/8″	1	7/32″	15	3/16″	12

ABRASIVE SELECTION CHART FOR POWER SANDERS

ABRASIVE	USE	GRIT		
		ROUGH	MEDIUM	FINE
Aluminum oxide	Hardwood	2 1/2–1 1/2	1/2–1/0	2/0–3/0
	Aluminum	1 1/2	1/2–0	2/0
	Copper	1 1/2–1	0–2/0	2/0–3/0
	Steel	3–2 1/2	1/2–0	2/0
	Ivory	1/2–0	2/0–3/0	2/0–8/0
	Plastics	1–0	3/0–5/0	7/0
Garnet	Hardwood	2 1/2–1 1/2	1/2–1/0	2/0–3/0
	Softwood	1 1/2–1	1/0	2/0
	Composition board	1 1/2–1	1/2	1/0
	Plastics	1–0	3/0–5/0	7/0
	Horn	1 1/2	1/2–0	2/0–3/0
Silicon carbide	Glass	1–1/2	2/0–3/0	4/0–8/0
	Cast iron	3–2 1/2	1/2–0	2/0
	Ceramics	1/2	3/0	4/0–8/0
	Gemstones	1–1/2	0–3/0	4/0–8/0
	Steel	3–2 1/2	1/2–0	2/0
	Plastics	1–0	3/0–5/0	7/0
Flint	Removing paint or old finishes	3–1 1/2	1/2–1/0	

GRIT EQUIVALENTS

8/0—280	5/0—180	2/0—100	1—50	2 1/2—30
7/0—240	4/0—150	0— 80	1 1/2—40	3—24
6/0—220	3/0—120	1/2— 60	2—36	

NUMBERING SYSTEM—TYPES OF PAPER

NAME DESIGNATIONS, ALL TYPES OF PAPER	ALUMINUM OXIDE OR SILICON OXIDE	GARNET	FLINT
Superfine	10/0—400	10/0—400	
Extra fine	9/0—320	9/0—320	
	8/0—280	8/0—280	
	7/0—240	7/0—240	
Very fine	6/0—220	6/0—220	4/0
	5/0—180	5/0—180	3/0
	4/0—150	4/0—150	2/0
Fine	3/0—120	3/0—120	
	2/0—100	2/0—100	0
Medium	0 — 80	0 — 80	1/2
	1/2— 60	1/2— 60	1
Coarse	1 — 50	1 — 50	1 1/2
	1 1/2— 40	1 1/2— 40	2
Very coarse	2 — 36	2 — 36	2 1/2
	2 1/2— 30	2 1/2— 30	3
	3 — 24	3 — 24	

AVERAGE FURNITURE, DIMENSIONS

ITEM	LENGTH, INCHES	DEPTH-WIDTH, INCHES	HEIGHT, INCHES
Dining table	60	42	29
Kitchen table	42	30	30
Card table	36	36	30
Coffee table	36–60	18–24	14–18
Coffee table (round)	36 diam.		15–18
End table	24	15	24
Drum table	36 diam.		30
Lamp table	24 diam.		30
Desk	48	24	30
Secretary	36	24	84
Lowboy	30	18	30
Highboy	36	18	60–84
Breakfront bookcase	48–60	18	78–84
Sofa	72	30	36
Love seat	48	30	36
Occasional chair	27	30	36
Occasional chair (armless)	24	30	30
Wing chair	30	30	36
Dining, desk, folding chair	15–18	15–18	30–36 (seat height 16–18)
Twin bed	78	39	20–24
Double bed	78	54	20–24
Dresser	42–60	22	32–36

COMMON NAILS

SIZE	LENGTH	DIAMETER GAUGE NO.	DIAMETER OF HEAD	APPROX. NO. PER POUND
2d	1″	15	11/64″	830
3d	1¼″	14	13/64″	528
4d	1½″	12½	¼″	316
5d	1¾″	12½	¼″	271
6d	2″	11½	17/64″	168
7d	2¼″	11½	17/64″	150
8d	2½″	10¼	9/32″	106
9d	2¾″	10¼	9/32″	96
10d	3″	9	5/16″	69
12d	3¼″	9	5/16″	63
16d	3½″	8	11/32″	49
20d	4″	6	13/32″	31
30d	4½″	5	7/16″	24
40d	5″	4	15/32″	18
50d	5½″	3	½″	14
60d	6″	2	17/32″	11

FINISHING NAILS

SIZE	LENGTH	DIAMETER GAUGE NO.	DIAMETER OF HEAD GAUGE NO.	APPROX. NO. PER POUND
2d	1″	16½	13½	1351
3d	1¼″	15½	12½	807
4d	1½″	15	12	584
5d	1¾″	15	12	500
6d	2″	13	10	309
8d	2½″	12½	9½	189
10d	3″	11½	8½	121
16d	3½″	11	8	90
20d	4″	10	7	62

GLOSSARY

ABRASIVE: Material such as sand-paper, pumice, or emery, used for polishing, sanding, and grinding.

ABRASIVE PAPER: Paper covered on one side with a substance used for grinding, sanding, or polishing.

ABRASIVE WHEEL: A grinding wheel made of emery or other abrasive material.

ACOUSTICAL TILES: Ceiling tile that aids hearing.

ACOUSTICS: Having to do with the transmission and reception of sound.

ACROSS THE GRAIN: At right angles to the run of the wood grain.

ADHESIVE: A medium, such as glue or cement, by which surfaces or ojjects are held together.

AIR DRIED: Lumber that has been seasoned in the air rather than in a kiln.

ANCHOR: To secure one object to another; a device used to attach two objects together.

ANGLE IRON: A piece of iron or metal in the shape of a right angle; used to reinforce joints.

ANNULAR RINGS: The irregular rings revealed in a cross section of a tree or timber which indicates yearly growth.

ASBESTOS SHINGLES: Roofing or siding shingles made of asbestos fibers and cement.

ASPHALT: A natural, bituminous substance of tar base used generally for waterproofing or combined with colored granules for roofing.

ASPHALT TILE: Square flooring material made of asphalt and available in many colors.

AUGER BIT: A twist drill bit used to bore large holes.

BACK BAND: The outside member of a window or door casing, rabbetted to receive the outside edge of the case.

BALUSTER: Vertical support for a handrail; a banister.

BALUSTRADE: A row of balusters topped by a rail; banisters.

BAND: Any flat, decorative or protective strip, set flush with or projecting above a surface.

BANISTER: Common term for baluster; vertical supports of stairway handrail.

BAR CLAMP: A steel or wood bar to which two movable jaws are attached, one actuated by a screw and one held in place by a spring hook fitting into notches on the bar.

BASEBOARD: A flat piece of finished lumber frequently molded on one edge and from four to eight inches in height. It is installed to provide a finish at junction of wall and floor and to protect the lower edge of the wall.

BATTEN: A narrow strip of wood nailed over joints of boards or ply-wood panels.

BATTEN BOARD: A hidden, wooden member to which other wooden members are attached.

BEAD: A rounded decorative molding with a small groove.

BEADING: Small wooden molding used for decorative purposes.

BEAM: A large structural member transversely supporting a load. An example is a beam under the floor of a house.

BEARING: That portion of a beam, truss, etc., that rests on the supports.

BEARING PARTITION (OR WALL): A partition or wall which supports any vertical load in addition to its own weight.

BEVEL: To cut on a slant, so the angle formed is not a right angle.

BEVEL SIDING: Siding made by "resawing" dry, square-surfaced boards diagonally to produce two wedge-shaped pieces. It is used as the finish siding on the exterior of a house.

BIRD'S MOUTH: The seat cut at the end of a rafter to fit the wall plate.

BLEED: Wood is said to bleed when the liquid contained in it works its way to the surface.

BOARD: Sawed thin lumber, longer than it is wide.

BOARD FOOT: A unit of measurement. It refers to a piece of lumber measuring one square foot on the surface and one inch in thickness.

BRACE: A support used to reinforce a structure.

BRAD: A thin wire nail with a small head.

BRIDGING: Small crossed members usually placed betwen floor joists to keep them in an upright position and to stiffen the floor above.

BUILDING CODE: A collection of legal requirements the purpose of which is to protect the safety, health and general welfare of those in and about buildings.

BUILDING PAPER: Waterproofed heavy paper applied over the rough sheathing of a house before shingles or other siding are added.

BUILT-UP TIMBER: Lumber made of several pieces of timber fastened together and forming one of larger dimension.

BUTT: To join end to end without overlapping.

BUTT JOINT: A joint formed by fastening parts together end to end without overlapping.

BUTT MITER: A surface beveled at an angle of 45°, joined with a similar surface and not overlapping.

CALIPERS: A tool similar to a draftsman's compass, used for measuring outside or inside diameters.

CASED: Closed in; a door or window opening after the trim has been fastened around a frame.

CASING: The trim around doors and windows.

C-CLAMPS: A hand clamp, shaped like the letter C, by which pressure is applied with a thumb screw.

CEILING: That covering of a room which hides the joists of the floor above or the rafters of the roof.

CEILING JOISTS: Lumber used to support the ceiling.

CHAIR RAIL: A wooden molding fastened to a wall at chair-back height to prevent damaging of the wall when chairs are pushed back.

CHAMFER: A sloping or beveled edge.

CHECK: A crack in a piece of lumber caused by very rapid drying or by natural causes.

CLAPBOARD: Board having one edge thicker than the other. Used for exterior siding of houses.

CLEAT: A piece of wood or metal screwed or nailed across the back of a panel to brace it against buckling; a short piece of wood fastened to a wall to support the end of a shelf.

CLINCH: To fasten securely.

CLOSE GRAIN: A compact arrangement of fibers in a piece of wood, especially hardwood, making it easy to dress and give a fine finish.

COARSE GRAIN: A loose arrangement of the fibers in a piece of wood, especially softwood, which is hard to dress and finish.

COAT: A protective or decorative layer of paint, shellac or other finish on wood or metal.

CORK TILE: A flooring material made of ground cork bark.

CORNER POST: The timbers forming the framed corner of a frame house.

CORNICE: The projection at the top of a wall finished by a blocking-course. Usually, the portion of a wall directly under the eaves.

COUNTERSINK: To drive nail heads below a surface or make depressions for screw heads, so that they will be below the surface of the wood in which they are inserted.

COVE: Concave molding.

CROSS CUTTING: Sawing wood across the grain.

CROSS LAP JOINT: A method of joining wooden members, at an angle, usually 90°, by removing half the thickness of each member so that the members lie in the same plane.

CULLS: Rejected material not fit for first-class work.

CUT: To divide or separate with a sharp instrument.

CUTTING EDGE: The sharp edge of any tool by which the cutting is done.

DADO: A rectangular, flat-bottomed groove cut in wood.

DADO JOINT: A joint made where one member fits into a dado cut in the other member.

DORMER: A built-up window structure projecting from a sloping roof.

DOVETAIL: A flaring-shaped tenon.

DOVETAIL JOINT: A method of fastening together, especially in cabinet work, by a system of interlocking tenons cut in dovetail form.

DOWEL: Pin which fits into a hole in an abutting piece and prevents slipping.

DOWEL JOINT: A joint made by gluing a dowel into two pieces of wood.

DRESSING: The operation of squaring and smoothing lumber.

DRY-WALL CONSTRUCTION: Any interior wall or ceiling material that does not have to be mixed with water before it can be applied. A plaster wall or ceiling, on the other hand, is called *wet-wall construction.*

DUTCH DOOR: A door so constructed that the upper or lower part can be shut while the other part remains open.

EAVES: That portion of the roof which extends beyond the walls.

EDGE GRAIN: Lumber sawed so that the wide surfaces extend approximately at right angles to the rings of growth.

EDGING: The decoration forming an edge or border.

END-MATCH LUMBER: Boards having the ends as well as the sides tongued and grooved.

FACE: The front or principal side of a building; surface of an object, a working face from which other surfaces or faces are trued.

FACE MOLD: A pattern for making the board from which ornamental hand railings and other works are to be cut.

FACE NAILING: To nail perpendicular to the initial surface or to the junction of the pieces being joined.

FACING: Any trim used to cover edges of an exterior finish.

FASCIA BOARD: A board fastened to the ends of the rafters forming part of a cornice.

FASTENING: Anything used in making an object secure, such as nails, screws, bolts, rivets or adhesive.

FIBERBOARD: An insulating lath or wall board of compressed fiber made from various kinds of vegetable matter, such as corn or sugar cane stalks.

FILLER: A material used to fill wood pores.

FINISH: The surface of an object when work on it has been completed.

FISH JOINT: A splice where two pieces are joined butt-end to end. The connection is made by pieces of wood or iron placed on each side and firmly bolted to the timbers or other pieces being joined.

FLAGSTONE: Large flat paving stone from one to two inches thick.

FLASHING: Material, usually lead, copper or zinc, used to waterproof joints between roof and chimneys; dormers or gables.

FLIGHT: A run of steps or stairs from one landing to another.

FLOORING: The whole structure of the floor of a building, including the supporting timbers.

FLUSH: Even, on a level, with an adjacent surface.

FLUTE: A channel or curved portion forming one of the several grooves in classical decoration.

FLUTING: A series of decorative flutes.

FOOTING: The lowest layers of material used in the foundation of a house which are wider than the foundation wall in order to carry the load.

FOUNDATION: The base upon which the building rests.

FRAME: The rough timbers of a house cut and assembled according to plan, including joints, girders, sells, corner posts, studs, plates and rafters. Also to fit and adjust, to join together.

FRAMING SYSTEMS: *BALLOON FRAMING:* A system of framing a building in which all vertical structural elements of the exterior walls, particularly the studs, consist of single pieces extending from the foundation sill to the roof plate, and support intermediate floor and ceiling joists. *BRACED FRAMING:* A system of framing a building in which all vertical structural elements of the bearing walls and partitions, except corner posts, extend for one story only, starting at the foundation sill for the first-story framing and at the top plate of the story below for all stories above the first. Corner posts extend from foundation sill to roof plate and are braced by diagonal members usually extending the full height of each story and crossing several of the studs in each outer wall. *PLATFORM FRAMING:* A system of framing a building on which floor joists of each story rest on the top plates of the story below (or on the foundation sill for the first story) and the bearing walls and partitions rest on the subfloor of each story.

FURRING: Strips of wood, brick, or metal usually one inch by two inches, fastened to a wall to make a straight or level surface to which plywood or other covering is fastened.

GABLE: Triangular wall surface formed at the end of a pitched roof.

GAIN: A notch or groove made across the grain in a piece of lumber to receive a second member.

GIRDER: Supporting member which spans an opening and carries a load or is subject to transverse stresses.

GLASS BLOCK: Translucent or transparent blocks of glass used in building.

GLAZED BRICK: Bricks with a glazed surface.

GLUE: An adhesive material.

GLUE BLOCK: A square or triangular block of wood glued and set into the interior angle formed by two boards to strengthen the joint.

GLUE JOINT: A joint formed by two boards to which glue has ben applied to hold them together.

GOUGE: A concave chisel-shaped cutting tool.

GRAIN: The pattern or direction of the fibers in a piece of wood, such as straight, open, close, cross, curly or short grain.

GRAINING: The process of imitating in a painted or stained surface the grain of wood, marble, etc; usually done with cloth, combs or rollers.

GREEN LUMBER: Lumber that has not been properly seasoned.

GRILLE: An ornamental, openwork, metal guard or grating to protect windows and other openings.

GRINDING: Removal of metal or other hard substances by means of drills or rigid wheels through friction.

GRINDSTONE: A circular sandstone which may be revolved for grinding, smoothing, and sharpening tools.

GRIT: Sandlike particles.

GROOVE: A term used to signify a sunken channel whose section is rectangular. It is usually used on the edge of a molding, stile, or rail, etc., into which a tongue corresponding to its section, and in the substance of the wood to which it is joined, is inserted.

HALF LAP JOINT: A joint used in splicing boards in which one half the thickness of each board is removed, permitting the boards to fit closely and to be firmly joined.

HALF-ROUND: A molding, semi-circular in shape or cross section.

HALVING: The joining of two pieces of timber by letting one into the other.

HANDRAIL: A rail or guard on a stair which may or may not be supported by posts or balusters.

HARDBOARD: Panel building material made by pressing wood fibers into thin ($\frac{1}{8}$ or $\frac{1}{4}$ inch) sheets.

HARDWARE: Metal ware, including locks, hinges, tools, nails, screws, etc.

HARDWOOD: Wood of hard texture and close grain, obtained from broad-leaved trees, such as beech, birch, maple, ash, hickory, oak, etc. The term refers to a botanical grouping and not to the actual hardness of the wood.

HEAD: Top member of door or window frame.

HEADER: The upper member of a rough window or door frame opening, usually two timbers laid on edge.

HEEL: End cut on a rafter. The foot of the rafter that rests on the wall plate.

HEELING: The action of saw blade teeth when they are not cutting in a true plane. In effect, the back teeth of the cutting blade are not following the plane (kerf) of the front teeth.

HINGE: A metal joint on which doors, covers, blinds, etc., swing, fold, open or close.

HIP: The external angle formed by the intersection of two sloping roof surfaces.

HIPPED ROOF: A roof which has ends formed by sloping faces.

HONEYCOMB PANEL: A structural wall material having cells suggesting a hive built by the honeybee.

HUNG: Suspended, as a door fitted into place with hinges.

INLAY: To cut out a surface to desired pattern and insert a different material for ornamental purposes.

INSULATING BOARD: A commercial product made of vegetable matter such as sugar cane or corn stalks, hemlock, spruce, or fir pulpwood fibers which are heated, "blown up," then pressed into boards or panels. Some may be used for both insulating and decorative applications.

JAMB: Vertical members of a door, window, or fireplace framework.

JIG: A device employed to simplify the operation of a power tool; a template used in producing numerous shapes of the same kind.

JOINERY: Skilled work in wood, such as cabinet work, furniture, building, etc.

JOINT: The point at which two pieces of material are joined to one another.

JOIST: One of a series of parallel beams used to support floor and ceiling loads, and supported in turn by larger beams, girders or bearing walls.

KERF: A cut or groove made by the saw blade in sawing.

KILN-DRIED: Term used to describe material that has been seasoned in a kiln oven rather than in the air.

KNOT: A hard section interrupting the grain of a piece of wood.

LAMINATED CONSTRUCTION: Any working member built up in layers to secure greater strength.

LAMINATED PLASTIC: Hard surface decorative material used for counter tops, table tops, etc.

LAP DOVETAIL: A joint used in drawer fronts, in which the dovetail is not exposed on the front of the drawers.

LAPPED JOINT: A joint made by cutting away half the thickness from the face of one piece and half the thickness from the back of another, thus making the surfaces flush when joined.

LATHS: Thin strips of wood nailed to studding as supports for plaster. Also, wire-mesh or composition plasterboard.

LATTICE: Any work of wood or metal that is made by crossing laths, rods, or bars to form a decorative network. Also may be cut from boards.

LEDGER STRIP: A strip of lumber nailed along the bottom of the side of a girder on which joists rest.

LINTEL: A horizontal structural member which supports the load over an opening such as a door or window.

LOUVER: A window-type ventilator, partially closed with slats set at an angle.

LUMBER: Sawed parts of a log such as boards, planks, scantling, and timber.

MARBLE: A type of crystalline limestone capable of taking a high polish, found in various colors caused by impurities.

MARQUETRY: Furniture or flooring having inlaid wood of various colors.

MASTIC: A type of composition cement used for linoleum, plastic and asphalt products.

MATCHED BOARDS: Boards cut with tongue and groove.

MEMBERS: The different parts of a building structure.

MILL WORK: Woodwork, trim, moldings, etc., finished by woodworking machines.

MITER: To fit together at an angle to form a miter joint.

MITER JOINT: A joint made by cutting two members at an angle and fitting them together, generally forming a 90° angle.

MOLDING: A narrow decorative strip applied to a surface.

MORTISE: A hole cut into a piece of wood to receive a tenon or tongue shaped at the end of another piece of wood. The resulting fit is called a *mortise and tenon joint*.

MULLION: A vertical bar or division in a sash frame in which two or more sashes are hung. Also a vertical member between the rails in a piece of framing.

NAIL SET: A steel tool used in sinking the head of a nail below the surface of the wood.

NON-BEARING PARTITION (OR WALL): A partition or wall extending from floor to ceiling which supports no load other than its own weight.

NOSING: The rounded edge on a stair tread or other projecting surface.

NOSING STRIP: A bull-nosed shape of stock placed as trim on a board, tread, etc.

NOTCH: A groove cut in a board into which another board may be inserted.

NOTCHED JOINT: A joint in which two boards crossing at right angles are gained or notched to prevent lateral movements.

NOVELTY SIDING: Wood siding cut into special designs.

ON CENTER: From center of one board to center of another.

OPEN GRAIN: The loose grain in a soft wood board which is easily torn or lifted when planing.

PANEL: A finished board enclosed in a frame; a decorative design on a wall or paper to represent a panel; a sheet of plywood, fiberboard, insulation board, hardboard, etc.; a raised or sunken section in a wall, ceiling, wainscoting, or door.

PARQUET: Hard wood blocks laid in geometric designs over a sub-floor.

PENNY: A measure of nail length and is abbreviated by the letter "d."

PERFORATE: To make holes, as to bore holes in a board.

PIER: A post of brick, masonry, concrete or metal to support beams or as part of a wall to add strength to a place where it is needed.

PITCH: The slope of a surface, such as a roof or stairs. Also an accumulation of resin in the wood cells.

PIVOT: A pin or point on which anything rotates.

PLANE: To make smooth.

PLASTERBOARD: A wall covering composed of prepared material in sheets of various sizes.

PLASTIC WOOD: A mixture of wood and adhesive plastics in putty form, used for patching blemishes in wood articles, floors, trim, etc.

PLATE: The timber that supports the end of the rafters in a building.

PLOUGH: To cut a groove running in the same direction as the grain of the wood.

PLUMB: To test a piece of work with level, plumb bob, or try square to see if it is perpendicular to the adjoining side.

PLYWOOD: A piece of wood made of three or more layers of thin sheets of wood or veneer joined with glue and usually laid with the grain of adjoining plies at right angles.

PRIMER: Thin undercoat of paint or wood finish, applied to fill pores and provide a base for additional coats.

PULLS: Wooden or metal handles usually attached at two points, for opening drawers.

QUARTER-ROUND: A plain molding showing a quarter circle in section.

RABBET: A rectangular recess cut on the face or edge of any material so that it may receive another member. Also to break or cover a joint, as in rabbeted doors, door jambs, etc.

RABBETED JOINT: A joint formed by two boards, rabbeted on opposite sides.

RAFTER: One of a series of structural members of a roof designed to support roof loads.

RAIL: A piece of metal or timber extending from one post to another, as in fences, balustrades, staircases, etc. In framing and paneling, the horizontal pieces are called *rails;* the perpendicular, *stiles.*

RAISED PANEL: The face of the panel is above the face of the framing.

RANDOM LENGTHS: Pieces of lumber varying in length.

RANDOM WIDTHS: Pieces of lumber varying in width.

RE-SAW: To saw a piece of timber already cut to dimensions, as in cutting boards from a squared timber.

RETURN: The continuation of a molding or finish of any kind in a different direction.

RIDGE: The highest point of a pitched roof, running the length of the roof.

RIPPING: Sawing wood with the grain or along the length of the wood.

RISER: The vertical part of a step.

ROOF: The entire construction used to enclose the top of a building.

ROOFING: The material put on a roof to make it watertight.

ROSETTE: An ornament in the form of a rose, used extensively in decoration.

ROUGH LUMBER: Lumber that has not been surfaced or dressed.

ROUT: To plow out or to gouge out.

SADDLE: The threshhold plate of a doorway.

SASH: The framework which holds the glass in a window.

SCANTLING: Lumber with a cross section ranging from two by four inches to four by four inches.

SCARFING: Joining and bolting two pieces of lumber together transversely so that the two appear to be one.

SCORE: To make notches or incisions along a cutting line.

SCRIBING: The marking of a piece of wood to provide for the fitting of one of its surfaces to the irregular surface of another.

SCROLLWORK: Any ornamentation featuring a scroll design; any thin wood cut into designs with a saber saw.

SEASONING: The process of removing moisture from wood either by natural or artificial means.

SEAT CUT: The cut at the bottom end of a rafter which rests upon the top of the plate. (Sometimes called a *plate cut.)*

SHAKES: Imperfections in timbers caused during the growth of a tree by high winds or other imperfect conditions.

SHEATHING: Tongued and grooved boards nailed directly to the wall frames and roof structure and used to furnish a backing for the exterior finish of a house. Also structural insulating board or wall board covering wall studs or rafters.

SHIM: A strip of material used to fill a small space.

SHINGLES: A finished roof or wall covering of wood, slate, asbestos, asphalt, etc.

SHIPLAP: Boards cut along the edge in such a fashion that when nailed alongside one another they form a half-lap joint.

SIDING: Shaped and finished boards used to cover the exterior walls. Sometimes made of asbestos, composition board, or wood in the form of clapboard, bevel, or shingles.

SILL: Bottom horizontal member of windows, doors, or framework.

SLIP STONE: A small wedge-shaped oil stone or carborundum piece used to sharpen tools.

SLOT: A long narrow groove or opening, as a mortise.

SOFTWOOD: The wood obtained from needle–leaved (coniferous) trees such as redwood, tamarack, spruce, fir, cypress, cedar, larch, etc.

SOLE PLATE: A horizontal member on which wall and partition studs rest.

SPLICE: To join two pieces of wood or other material lengthwise by beveling, scarfing, overlapping or entwining.

SPLICED JOINT: A joint that has been formed by lapping materials at the corners or end.

SPLINE: A thin piece of wood placed in a miter joint after the miters have been grooved in order to strengthen the joint.

SPLINED JOINT: A tongued and grooved joint formed by placing a loose strip of wood or metal in the grooves formed on the edge of adjoining boards.

STEP: That portion of a stairway consisting of the tread and riser.

STOP: A strip of wood fastened to the jambs and head of a door frame against which the door closes.

STRAIGHTEDGE: A board or piece of metal having edges parallel and straight.

STRING: The sloping support for the steps of a stairway.

STUD: One of a series of vertical supporting members of a framework or partition. Also, a nail with a large head.

SUB-FLOOR: The rough floor nailed to the floor joists.

SURFACED LUMBER: Lumber that has been dressed.

TEMPLATE: A thin piece of metal or board used as a pattern. Also, a supporting bridge in construction.

TENON: A projection on the end of a piece of wood which is fitted into a mortise.

TERRAZZO: A mosaic without formal pattern, formed by small pieces of marble, glass or pottery embedded in cement and ground down to a smooth, even surface.

THICKNESS: The distance between the two broad surfaces.

THRESHOLD: The piece of wood, stone or metal which lies under a door or the sill of a door.

TILES: Small squares of ceramic, plastic, metal, asphalt, cork, etc., used for wall and floor covering.

TIMBER: Lumber with a cross section over four by six inches, such as posts, sills, and girders.

TOENAILING: To drive a nail at an angle to the initial surface in order to permit penetration into a second member.

TONGUE: A rib on the edge of a board that fits into a groove on the edge of another board to make a flush joint.

TREAD: The upper horizontal part of a step.

TRIM: The finish materials in a building, such as moldings applied around openings (window trim), or at the floor and ceiling of rooms.

TRUE: To make even, to level.

VALANCE: A decorative device across the top of a window from behind which draperies are hung.

VALLEY: The internal angle formed by two inclined sides of a roof.

VENEER: A thin layer of wood glued to a base made of a cheaper or inferior wood.

WAINSCOTING: Covering the lower part of interior walls with wooden paneling.

WALL BOARD: Wood pulp, gypsum or similar materials made into large, rigid sheets that may be fastened to the frame of a building to provide a surface finish.

WIDTH: The distance across the grain on the broadest surface.

NO-TIME-LIMIT
(B-D) Quality Guarantee

Every Black & Decker product has been carefully inspected before shipment, and we guarantee to correct any defect caused by faulty material or workmanship. Our obligation assumed under this guarantee is limited to the replacing of any part or parts which prove to our satisfaction, upon examination, to have been defective and which have not been misused or carelessly handled. The complete unit must be returned to one of our Factory Service Branches, Authorized Service Stations or to our Factory, transportation charges prepaid. We reserve the right to decline responsibility where repairs or replacements have been made or attempted by others. No other guarantee, written or verbal, is authorized on our products.

Happy Woodworking!

The Black & Decker Manufacturing Company • Towson, Maryland 21204

Designed and produced by Western Printing and Lithographing Company
in co-operation with The Black & Decker Manufacturing Company
Printed in U.S.A.